Praise for *Innovation Games*

"*Innovation Games* is one of those books you don't know you need until you read it, and then you wonder how you ever got along without it. If you hope to have customers tomorrow, you need to read this book and play these games!"

—Michael J. Hunter
Test Technical Lead, Microsoft Expression

"Luke's book fills a gap in the bookshelf—we have too many books on how to build a product, and not enough on learning what to build in the first place."

—Alistair Cockburn
Humans and Technology

"*Innovation Games* is a refreshing return to the customer perspective as the primary driver of innovation. By directly engaging customers with Luke's 'games,' solution-providers will build better relationships with their customers while learning about real pain points. Luke has balanced a unique mix of market research techniques with fun, team-building exercises—creating a better fit between innovators and their customers."

—Dave Weinerth
Director, Business Development, Palo Alto Research Center Incorporated

"I had the opportunity to experience one of the Innovation Games, Prune the Product Tree, at the Product Management Educational Conference 2006. Because it was presented as a game, a group of us—complete strangers at the start—quickly became involved and engaged in suggesting improvements and changes. This game makes it easy to generate simpler, standalone suggestions, all while helping you keep the big picture in mind. These games are a faster and more effective way to get high-quality input from your market."

—Jacques Murphy
Editor, Product Management Challenges Newsletter, www.ProductManagementChallenges.com

"I ran the Buy a Feature game at our 2004 user group, 'Agility.' The experience was enlightening and useful for both myself, as a product manager, and our customers. I was quite pleased with our customers' responses following the event. One person said, 'I'm honored you invited me (us) to this event and hope you continue to do this in the future.' Another said, 'This was the greatest experience I've ever seen your company do for customers. I'd like to participate in the next session.' As a result of playing the game, I felt I had a more validated list of customer requirements than before and I felt that my credibility behind these requirements was not challenged. It was truly empowering and I wish anyone who attempts to use Innovation Games the best success. It's worth every ounce of effort!"

—Brian Cipresse
Director, PC/EC Agile Software Corporation

"The use of Enthiosys' Innovation Games at our Technical Advisory Council meetings have not only provided us with wonderful insights regarding product strategies, requirements, and new market opportunities, more importantly they have given our customers new and creative ways to provide feedback in a way that they enjoy."

—Neal Starling
Vice President Sales and Service, Emerson Climate Technologies

"I highly recommend contracting with Luke and his team to help your Product Management organization run this type of event. He and his games structure the events so well that great results are almost guaranteed."

—Ryan Martens
President, Rally Software Development

"Continuous innovation is hard. Continuously innovating the right products, features, and capabilities is even harder. After seeing these Innovation Games in action with real customers driving the development of real products, I am convinced that Luke has created a better way to ensure that customers get what they truly want. These games are fun for customers. But more importantly, they get customers thinking in unique and unusual ways, which leads to better innovation."

—Ken Collier, PhD
President, KWC Technologies, Inc.

"Luke Hohmann had his students critique SD West at SD West in his tutorial on Innovation Games. I received lots of great feedback from the group. If you're interested in improving your product, there's no better inspiration (or source of information) than your customer."

—Tamara Carter Sriram
Conference Manager, SD Events, CMP Media

"Luke has come up with a variety of innovative ways to invoke your customer into helping you improve your product, focus your product development, develop stronger customer relations, and save you time and money by delivering what your customers want. The techniques employed by the Innovation Games span creativity both on the part of the customer and the developer. Better, more focused products are the result."

—Don Gray
President, Sales Engineering Group

"One of the most difficult tasks of a product manager is to understand customer needs and translate them into product features. This book not only makes this task fun and entertaining, but also easy to accomplish. The approaches are straightforward and make so much sense that I kept on finding myself saying, 'Now why didn't I think of that before?' Through his Innovative Games, Luke Hohmann does a magnificent job in harnessing and enticing customers to help product teams understand their customers in return."

—Laila Arad-Allan
Senior Product Manager, Software DRM, Aladdin Knowledge Systems

"The purpose of this book is found in its title: 'Creating Breakthrough Products.' The 'Games' or interactive discussions Luke Hohmann offers will help anyone who is truly interested in discovering what the customer wants versus what the customer says they want or worse, what you think they should want. The 'Innovation' will emerge if the practitioner is patient and follows Luke's facilitation suggestion to 'remember that your primary goal is to gain a better understanding of your customer.' These techniques do work!"

—David Spann
CEO, Agile—Adaptive Management, Certified Professional Facilitator

"Ever wonder where those software requirements and user stories come from? Hohmann provides practical techniques to help software teams develop insights into the real business needs and opportunities their solutions are intended to address. A unique and innovative work that will help software teams on their quest to build better software; software that is indeed a better 'fit for its intended purpose.'"

—Dean Leffingwell
Software Business Advisor, Executive and Author of *Managing Software Requirements* (Addison-Wesley, 2003)

"Customers have a hard time articulating breakthrough ideas when asked 'What do you want?' Luke's book offers practical, engaging activities to do with your customers to stimulate ideas and explore needs and wants that they can't clearly state. These ideas will lead to more innovative, compelling solutions, and he even has activities to give you insights into the value customers assign to the features or solutions."

—Barbara Nelson
Pragmatic Marketing Instructor, Practical Product Management and Requirements That Work

"Agile methods have provided a framework for improving innovation, but there has been a missing piece—and Luke Hohmann has helped fill in that blank space. *Innovation Games* offers ideas, tools, and practices to aid the innovation process at its most critical point—product management, particularly product visioning. The key to innovation isn't some stuffy process; it is creating a collaborative, interactive, visually-oriented, fun, business-value-driven environment in which people can generate, aggregate, and make decisions on ideas. Using the material in *Innovation Games* will greatly aid you in building such an environment."

—Jim Highsmith
Sr. VP and Director, Agile Software Development and Project Management Practice; Fellow, Business Technology Council Cutter Consortium LLC, Arlington, MA

"At our last customer advisory board, rather than the conventional force-field analysis and requirements discussion, we played two Innovation Games: Speed Boat and Prune the Product Tree. The results were far more interesting than previous years' results—particularly the tree exercise—and yielded compelling visual representations of the issues facing our customers and what in our product suite they considered essential components. I took the tree pruning drawings back to engineering and taped the pages to a conspicuous part of one wall (we used the kind of oversized paper you find on easels). The developers gathered around one by one as they noticed the drawings going up on the wall and puzzled over what it meant. For the next 30 minutes, we stood around and discussed the similarities between the drawings, the customers' needs and their perceptions of what was truly important, and where components fit 'organically.' The discussion was superb and fruitful, if you'll forgive the pun, because the information was so clearly represented as an image...a metaphor...that sticks in the mind with far more tenacity than paragraphs of text or bullet points summarizing the same material."

—Theron Davis
Product Manager, TetraData Corporation

"We all have different mental models of what our words and concepts mean to us—never mind what we think they mean to other people. And these models are difficult to communicate.... Luke Hohmann's book of reliable tools, which he calls Innovation Games, help make these mental models that consumers compose in their heads visible and tangible for them—and for you—to see and understand."

—Todd Siler, Ph.D.
Founder and Chief Creative Officer, Think Like a Genius, LLC

"Agile teams are now developing software more quickly than ever before. Unfortunately this doesn't mean they are always aimed at building the right products. This remarkable book will give you the tools you need to make sure your team is building exactly what your users need."

—Mike Cohn
Author of *Agile Estimating and Planning*

"I've used Luke's games with my customers, and their responses were more positive than any I've received for any other requirements activity I've used. The results of the games were immediately useful in shaping our team's product vision."

—David Kane

Innovation Games

Innovation Games

Creating Breakthrough Products Through Collaborative Play

Luke Hohmann

✦✦ Addison-Wesley

Upper Saddle River, NJ · Boston · Indianapolis · San Francisco
New York · Toronto · Montreal · London · Munich · Paris · Madrid
Cape Town · Sydney · Tokyo · Singapore · Mexico City

The publisher offers excellent discounts on this book when ordered in quantity for bulk purchases or special sales, which may include electronic versions and/or custom covers and content particular to your business, training goals, marketing focus, and branding interests. For more information, please contact:

U.S. Corporate and Government Sales
(800) 382-3419
corpsales@pearsontechgroup.com

For sales outside the United States please contact:

International Sales
international@pearsoned.com

Visit us on the Web: www.awprofessional.com

Library of Congress Cataloging-in-Publication Data

Hohmann, Luke.
  Innovation games : creating breakthrough products and services / Luke Hohmann.
    p. cm.
  ISBN 0-321-43729-2 (pbk. : alk. paper) 1. New products. 2. Production management. 3. Games. I. Title.
  TS170.H64 2006
  658.4'0353--dc22

                            2006019692

Pearson Education, Inc.
Rights and Contracts Department
75 Arlington Street, Suite 300
Boston, MA 02116
Fax: (617) 848-7047

ISBN 0-321-43729-2
Text printed in the United States on recycled paper at R. R. Donnelley in Crawfordsville, Indiana.
Sixth Printing, May 2011

I dedicate this book to my wife Jena, who believed in this book and gave me the time I needed to write it. Thank you, my love. This book would not exist without your help.

I also dedicate this book to everyone who wishes to create innovative products and services through better understanding of their customers. This book is for you.

CONTENTS

About the Author   xix

Foreword   xxi

Preface   xxiii

Acknowledgments   xxix

PART ONE: The Why and the How of Innovation Games   **1**

What Are Innovation Games?   2

Organizing and Using Innovation Games   6

    Organizing Innovation Games   6

    Four Ways to Use Innovation Games   7

Innovation Games as a Market Research Technique   7

    A Market Research Process   9

    Primary and Secondary Data   10

    Whom Do I Ask? Market Segmentation   12

    Questions, Data, Answers, and Actions   14

    The Unique Benefits (and Drawbacks) of Qualitative Market Research   15

What Makes Innovation Games Special?   16

The Innovation Games Process   18

Selecting the Right Innovation Game   20

    Degree of Open-Ended Exploration   20

    Number of Customers Who Can Play the Game   21

    Preparation Workload   22

    Time Frame of Action   24

Planning Your Innovation Game   26

    A Planning Timeline   26

    Phases of Preparation   27

Organizing Your Team   29

    The Day of Your Innovation Game   35

Processing the Results of Your Innovation Game   37

Innovation Games and Customer-Centric New Product Innovation Processes   40

    Ideation Phase   41

Customer-Centric Innovation Summary   43

Using Innovation Games to Feed Product Requirements   43

Using Innovation Games with Customer Advisory Boards   44

Summary   45

PART TWO: The Games   47

Prune the Product Tree   48

The Game   49

Why It Works   49

Preparing for the Game   49

    Materials   52

Playing the Game   52

Processing the Results   54

How I Can Use Prune the Product Tree   55

Remember the Future   56

The Game   57

Why It Works   57

Preparing for the Game   59

    Materials   59

Playing the Game   59

Processing the Results   61

How I Can Use Remember the Future   61

Spider Web   62

The Game   63

Why It Works   63

Preparing for the Game   64

    Materials   65

Playing the Game   66

Processing the Results   66

How I Can Use Spider Web   67

Product Box   68

The Game   69

Why It Works   69

Preparing for the Game   69

    Materials   71

Playing the Game   72

Processing the Results   74
How I Can Use Product Box   75

Buy a Feature   **76**
The Game   77
Why It Works   77
Preparing for the Game   77
    Materials   81
Playing the Game   81
Processing the Results   82
How I Can Use Buy a Feature   83

Start Your Day   **84**
The Game   85
Why It Works   86
Preparing for the Game   86
    Materials   87
Playing the Game   88
Processing the Results   89
How I Can Use Start Your Day   91

Show and Tell   **92**
The Game   93
Why It Works   93
Preparing for the Game   93
    Materials   94
Playing the Game   95
Processing the Results   95
How I Can Use Show and Tell   95

Me and My Shadow   **96**
The Game   97
Why It Works   97
Preparing for the Game   98
    Materials   98
Playing the Game   98
Processing the Results   100
How I Can Use Me and My Shadow   101

Give Them a Hot Tub   **102**
The Game   103
Why It Works   103

Preparing for the Game 103
    Materials 104
Playing the Game 104
Processing the Results 104
How I Can Use Give Them a Hot Tub 105

The Apprentice **106**
The Game 107
Why It Works 107
Preparing for the Game 107
    Materials 108
Playing the Game 108
Processing the Results 108
How I Can Use the Apprentice 109

20/20 Vision **110**
The Game 111
Why It Works 111
Preparing for the Game 112
    Materials 112
Playing the Game 112
Processing the Results 114
How I Can Use 20/20 Vision 117

Speed Boat **118**
The Game 119
Why It Works 119
Preparing for the Game 120
    Materials 120
Playing the Game 121
Processing the Results 123
How I Can Use Speed Boat 125

PART THREE: Tools and Templates **127**

Phase One Planning in Greater Detail 128
Customizing Games for Your Event 131
    Customizing *Speed Boat* 131
    Customizing *Product Box* 132
    Customizing *Buy a Feature* 132

Sample Agenda for an Innovation Game   133
  Purpose   133
  Background and Logistics   133
  Key Goals   133
  Key Remaining Action Items   134
  Room Layout and Customer Organization   135
  Detailed Schedule   136
Sample Invitation Letter   137
Thank You Letter Template   137
AirIT Sample Thank You Letter   137
Basic Materials Checklists   142
  Room   142
  Basic Materials for All Games   142
  Product Box Materials (per table)   142
  Buy a Feature Materials (per table)   142
  Start Your Day Materials   142
Frequently Asked Questions (FAQs)   144
Facilitating a Terrific Innovation Game Session   147
  Your Goal: Understanding   147
  Practice Before You Play   147
  Allow Plenty of Time for the Session   147
  Give Customers Time to Play the Game   147
  Quality, Not Quantity   148
  Play Quiet Music   148
  Email Can Wait   148
  Uh-oh...I Didn't Expect That   148
  Transcribe the Results   148
  Give Them Feedback   149
  Say Thank You   149
  Customize with Experience   149
  A Good Facilitator   149

Conclusion   **151**
Index   **153**

ABOUT THE AUTHOR

Luke Hohmann is the founder and CEO of Enthiosys, Inc., a Silicon Valley-based software product strategy and management consulting firm. Luke is also the author of *Beyond Software Architecture: Creating and Sustaining Winning Solutions* and *Journey of the Software Professional: A Sociology of Software Development*. Luke graduated magna cum laude with a B.S.E. in computer engineering and an M.S.E in computer science and engineering from the University of Michigan. While at Michigan he studied cognitive psychology and organizational behavior in addition to data structures and artificial intelligence. He is a former National Junior Pairs Figure Skating Champion and American College of Sports Medicine certified aerobics instructor. A member of the PDMA, ACM, and IEEE, in his spare time he enjoys roughhousing with his four kids, his wife's cooking, and long runs in the Santa Cruz mountains (because he really does enjoy his wife's cooking).

FOREWORD

by Joan Waltman, President, QUALCOMM Wireless Business Solutions

Having worked in the technology industry for the past 22 years, I have come to appreciate the uniqueness of true ground-breaking innovation and advancements that lead to changes in the way that people live their lives. Having worked for QUALCOMM for the past 16 of these 22 years, I have gained a deep appreciation for what it means to deliver 10X improvements through technological advancements and I have seen the corresponding improvement in quality of life that that can bring. QUALCOMM is a company renowned for both creating new science and technology (invention) and applying it to solve customer problems (innovation). As a result, I must admit that I was a bit skeptical when I heard that Luke would lead a session in which he would ask key customers of our FleetAdvisor fleet management system to describe the "anchors" holding down their FleetAdvisor system "boats." And then, when that was done, he would ask our customers to create a box representing their ideal FleetAdvisor system product so that they could "sell" it to us to

help us identify untapped market needs. Still, I thought that the idea sounded promising enough to give it a try. I'm glad we did.

That was several years ago. Since then, our division has leveraged several of these Innovation Games to help us do the following:

- Better understand how customers use our products, so that we can make effective roadmap and strategy decisions
- Identify key marketing messages for the launch of our asset-tracking product line
- Discover new product opportunities, resulting in the creation of our new business intelligence solution

As Luke and our QUALCOMM Wireless Business Solutions (QWBS) team "experimented" with learning customer preferences and needs through these games and tools, there have been times when a small number of our customers have reported that they were resistant to participating in the activities. Although this is disappointing, I feel that our commitment to serving our customers has been advanced through the use of Innovation Games. If you approach the use of these games and tools with an open mind and a similar commitment to understanding your customers, I think you will realize similar benefits. The key is matching the right game to the audience and preparing them appropriately for what they will be asked to do and how it will ultimately benefit them through the development of better products. Reading this book and participating in the forums will help you do this.

As time moves on, technologies advance ever more rapidly, and the longer lasting value of any technology is ultimately played out in how it becomes customized to suit different lifestyles, businesses, and personal preferences. As a result, I've come to believe that customer intimacy—having a deep sense of what customers do and how to translate that into technological innovation—is both an art and a science that creates competitive advantage. Because product developers typically are not also customers, and customers cannot tell you what they have not experienced or how future technological advancements could change their lives, finding ways to solve customers' unmet needs and problems in a meaningful way is always going to be a challenge. *Innovation Games: Creating Breakthrough Products Through Collaborative Play* presents many creative ways to gather those keen insights and nuggets of understanding that can make all the difference in deciding which problems you choose to solve for your customers and in how well you can achieve that ultimate goal of delivering superior products to the market.

Joan Waltman
President
QUALCOMM Wireless Business Solutions

PREFACE

Innovation Games are fun ways to collaborate with your customers to better understand their needs. You can use them to discover new business opportunities, drive strategy and product road map decisions, improve the effectiveness of sales and service organizations, fine-tune marketing messages, and create more intimate, durable relationships with your customers. You can also use them to better understand the people that you care about the most, from your family and friends to close business colleagues. To illustrate, here are ways some companies and people have used Innovation Games:

Understanding complex product relationships—When Wyse Technologies, Inc. wanted to gain a better understanding of how their customers perceived the business and technical relationships between the products and services provided by Wyse and those provided by other technology providers, they played *Spider Web* with a select group of customers at their Customer Advisory Board meeting.

Understanding product evolution—Rally Software Development had a more focused objective: they wanted specific feedback on

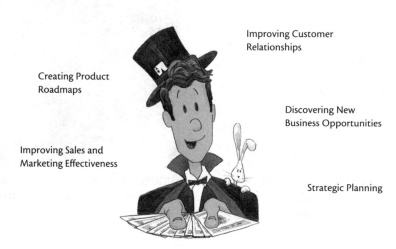

Creating Product Roadmaps

Improving Sales and Marketing Effectiveness

Improving Customer Relationships

Discovering New Business Opportunities

Strategic Planning

FIGURE 0.1 Innovation Games can be used to accomplish many kinds of goals.

how to prioritize features in upcoming product releases. After considering *Buy a Feature, 20/20 Vision,* and *Prune the Product Tree,* three games that help prioritize features, they ultimately chose *Prune the Product Tree* as the game that allowed them to best capture customer feedback on their development plans.

Understanding sales needs—QUALCOMM used *Product Box* in an internal sales training exercise to identify critical customer success factors and relate these to product benefits. Another company, Ticketmaster, used *Buy a Feature* in an internal sales meeting to prioritize the features that the sales team felt would help them accomplish their objectives.

Identifying areas for improvement—Aladdin Knowledge Systems, Inc., QUALCOMM, and Precision Quality Software have all used *Speed Boat* to identify key areas for improvement in their product and service offerings.

Prioritizing market needs—Emerson Climate Technologies provides the Intelligent Store, a broad and comprehensive architecture that combines unique equipment, software, and services to solve food safety, energy management, and facilities management needs. Emerson used *Spider Web*, *Speed Boat*, and *20/20 Vision* at their 2006 Technology Advisory Council meeting to better understand market needs relative to all aspects of the Intelligent Store.

Understanding hidden desires—Andre Gous's stepdaughter Karen was having trouble finding just the right used car. Andre runs Precision Quality Software and is a recognized expert on various software requirements engineering techniques. Andre tried using traditional requirements engineering to help her clarify her objectives. Unfortunately, after 45 minutes, they were no closer to the goal of defining her ideal car, and Karen was starting to become a little frustrated with the process. Andre tried *Product Box*, and in short order they had identified exactly what Karen was looking for in her "new" used car (you can read the entire story at the Innovation Games forum, www.innovationgames.com).

FIGURE 0.2 With a little imagination, Innovation Games can be used in countless situations.

Creating strategic plans—SDForum is the leading Silicon Valley not-for-profit organization providing an unbiased source of information and insight to the technology community for 20 years. Laura Merling, Executive Director of SDForum, used *Remember the Future* to create a five-year vision for how their organization will evolve to meet the needs of new technology entrepreneurs in Silicon Valley and around the world.

These stories illustrate the broad range in which people like you, for professional and personal reasons, are using Innovation Games. You can use Innovation Games to accomplish these and other goals. If you use these games, you'll come to understand what your customers really want. You'll have fun doing it. Perhaps more importantly, they'll have fun doing it. Armed with this understanding, you'll be able to create the breakthrough innovative products that are the foundation of lasting success. This book will show you how.

How This Book Is Organized

This book is organized into three parts.

Part One: The Why and the How of Innovation Games

Part One provides a comprehensive overview of Innovation Games. Starting with why you might want to play them in the first place, it will cover some of the different ways in which you can use the games and answer some of the common questions we get from people who are considering the games. Part One describes an easy-to-use process for selecting, planning, playing, and postprocessing the results of a game in ways that benefit you and your customers. This process has been used successfully in many games. At the end of Part One you'll have the foundation you need to move forward with one or more specific games.

Part Two: The Games

In Part Two you'll learn the details about each game, from "what makes the game work" to specific advice on planning, playing, and postprocessing the results. It is helpful to start by briefly skimming each game, making notes on how you might apply it. You'll probably find that one or two games catch your eye more than the others. This is not an accident; these are the games most likely to help you address your most pressing concerns. Go back to these games and carefully read each one in detail. When you're finished, you should have a good understanding of how these games can meet your needs and how to modify the general process described in Part One to put them in action. Along the way, by reading about how other companies have used them, you'll gain insight and inspiration about how you can apply these games.

Part Three: Tools and Templates

Part Three is designed to help you use Innovation Games by providing you with a variety of tools and templates to plan, play, and process the results of a game. It includes such things as sample invitation letters, general materials and supply checklists, advice on preparing event venues and facilitating the games, and frequently asked questions.

FORUM FOR READERS, GAME PLAYERS, AND FACILITATORS

In addition to this book, the people who use Innovation Games have found creative ways to extend them and are sharing their experiences with others at www.innovationgames. com. I invite you to join this community, share your own experiences, and provide help and encouragement to others. Most of all, have *fun* with what follows.

Luke Hohmann
Founder and CEO
Enthiosys, Inc.
lhohmann@enthiosys.com

THE ARTWORK

The artwork for the games was created by Brent Rosenquist. Brent has worked with me for a number of years in a variety of roles: developer, user interface designer, and graphic artist, to name just a few. He worked with Rhett Guthrie to design the cover art for my first book, *Journey of the Software Professional: A Sociology of Software Development.* He is an exceptionally accomplished software developer, a great artist, and a wonderful friend. I hope you like the art as much as I do.

The artwork used to describe how to play the games was created by Eliel Johnson. I met Eliel at the dcamp unconference, where he created one the most beautiful product boxes I've ever seen. I later learned that Eliel is an accomplished artist and user experience architect, with more than 10 years of experience working with Fortune 500 clients in the United States and Europe. He is a firm believer in a user-centered approach to design, and his passion about all aspects of innovation made him a natural choice to create the images you see in the book. You can learn more about Eliel at www.elieljohnson.com.

—Luke Hohmann

ACKNOWLEDGMENTS

I am deeply indebted to all of my clients who have worked with me over the years and who are the true pioneers in having fun learning about their customers. Many of them (okay, all of them!) had to make the same leap of faith that I'm asking you to make in reading this book—actually playing Innovation Games with your customers. It is my great honor to work for them.

I am equally indebted to the generosity of the many reviewers from around the world who worked to help me write the best book possible. First and foremost is my wife, Jena, who among so many other wonderful things that she does, gets the credit for tempering my use of rhetorical questions. Where would I be without her?

Other reviewers who have been so very helpful include (in alphabetical order) Dottie Acton, Sinan Si Alhir, Cliff Apsey, Paul Bain, Paul Becker, Greg Belaus, Steve Berczuk, Mark Better, Hugh R. Beyer, Lynn Bittner, Dave Brinkley, Sheri Byrne, Larry Cady, Mike Cohn, Philip Costa, dcamp attendees, Jordan Du Val, Bruce Eckfeldt, Nancy Frishberg, Scott Gilbert, Francine Gordon, Ellen Gottesdiener, Andre Gous, Donald Gray, Karen Gray (with a special mention for great editing), Bruce Griffin, Jeff Grigg, Jeff Griswold, Brent Harrison, Michael Hunter, Don Jarrell, Paul Jenkins, Dave J. Johansen, Steve Johnson, Christine Jorgenson, Cindy Lu, Ron Lunde, Tobias Mayer, Steve Meredith, Linda Merrick, Jacqueline Meyer, Steve Mezak, Jacquelyn Michel, Jeff Miller, Keith Mitchell, Tushar Montaño, Rick Mugridge, Dan Muto, Barbara Nelson, Jade Ohlhauser, Melisa Oldland, Steven Peacock, Kert Peterson, Scott Peterson, Tom Pittman, Andy Pols, Scott Pringle, Rob Purser, Dave Quick, Chuck Rabb, Charley Rego, Linda Rising, Doug Rybacki, Daryl Sconyers, Dharmesh Shah, Sharkidog, Daniel Shefer, the Silicon Valley Patterns Group, Dave W. Smith, David Spann, Dan Stadler, Gabriel Steinhardt, Susan Talarico, Larry Teslar, Lisa Teslar, Harold Thomas, Bill Trosky, Robert Vallelunga, William Wake, Anthony Williams, and Mike Young.

Very special thanks to the Enthiosys team for all their hard work in helping our clients create innovative products and services.

I'd like to thank Barbara Hacha for her superb copy editing, and Kim Scott for creating the terrific graphic layout for the book.

Finally, I am deeply thankful for the help of Michael Thurston, my book developer. He worked many long hours helping me organize and shape the material that is in this book. He did a stellar job.

I apologize, in advance, for anyone not explicitly acknowledged here.

—Luke Hohmann

Part One
THE WHY AND THE HOW OF INNOVATION GAMES

In the introduction you read stories of companies and people who apply Innovation Games to better understand their customers and in doing so solve a variety of problems associated with creating innovative products and services. Part One of this book gives you the foundation you need to use Innovation Games to accomplish your goals. It starts with an overview of Innovation Games, discusses how they can be used, and moves through the process of selecting, planning, playing, and processing the results of a game. It prepares you for Part Two, in which each game is discussed in greater detail.

WHAT ARE INNOVATION GAMES?

Innovation Games are fun ways to collaborate with your customers to better understand their needs. There are twelve Innovation Games explained in this book. Table 1.1 provides a brief description of each game.

Table 1.1   Innovation Games

Innovation Game		Description
Show and Tell		Customers describe the most important artifacts produced by your system to you and other customers.
Start Your Day		Customers collaboratively describe when, how, and where they use your product(s).
Prune the Product Tree		Customers work in small teams to shape the evolution of your products and services.
Me and My Shadow		Discover hidden needs by carefully observing what customers actually do with your products.
Product Box		Customers work individually or in small teams to create and sell their ideal product.
The Apprentice		Create empathy for the customer experience by doing the job of a customer.

Innovation Game		Description
Speed Boat		Customers identify their biggest pain points with your products and services.
Buy a Feature		Customers work together to purchase their most desired features.
20/20 Vision		Customers negotiate the relative importance of such things as product features, market requirements, and product benefits.
Spider Web		Customers work individually or in small teams to create vivid pictures of how your products and services fit into their world.
Give Them a Hot Tub		Customers provide feedback on outrageous features to establish what is truly essential.
Remember the Future		Understand your customers' definition of success by seeing how they shape their future.

To illustrate how you might use an Innovation Game, suppose you are an alarm clock radio manufacturer and your product team is interested in better understanding current and future market needs associated with a "next generation" clock radio.

You could accomplish this through any number of techniques. You could engage a simple and direct form of market research and simply ask your customers, "What do you want in your clock radio?" The answers may help your team, but your team may find the customers' responses relatively simplistic and lacking rich detail.

You could employ a significantly more advanced form of market research, such as a detailed questionnaire followed up with conjoint analysis. The result is more likely to be analytic ("47% of customers surveyed wanted a variable snooze timer, a way to wirelessly connect a personal computer to store MP3 files, and two alarms") but this approach can often feel sterile and suffers from a lack of discovery because you, and not your customers, have predetermined the set of features that are being explored.

Or you could play an Innovation Game, such as *Product Box*, with a representative group of customers. With *Product Box,* you would ask them to design their ideal clock radio, using blank cardboard boxes and fun supplies that you provide. When they had finished, you would ask them to sell their idealized creation to you and the other customers in the group.

FIGURE 1.1 Making a Product Box

FIGURE 1.2 Selling a Product Box

At the end of the game you would have a collection of product boxes that describe your customers' ideal clock radio. You would also have the rich descriptions of features and benefits associated with this idealized radio, and the questions and answers of other customers who were being "sold" this wonderful new device. You could then mine all of this for powerful insights, as I'll describe later in Part Two.

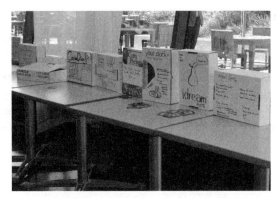

FIGURE 1.3 Gallery of Product Boxes

Overly Simplistic or Overly Complex Market Research

Innovation Games strike a balance between the overly simplistic and overly analytic approaches to trying to understand customers. Overly simplistic approaches rely too much on direct questioning, asking customers "What do you want?" (or its cousin, "What do you think our product should do?"). If you've asked these questions, you've probably come to realize that they tend to produce disappointing results. Customers are people. They often have trouble understanding their problems. And even if they think they understand their problems, and can describe them, that doesn't mean they can articulate the solutions they are seeking. Of course, many times they often don't know they had a problem, or that they desired a solution, until they see or possess it—much like I never knew how much I needed a Swiss+Tech Utili-Key until Todd Girvin, a friend who travels as much for his company as I do for mine, gave me one for my birthday! (The Swiss+Tech Utili-Key is a small, multifunction pocket knife that, when folded, resembles a key. You can put it on your key ring and continue to keep it there because it slides through the airport security screening process.)

At the other of the spectrum from simple questions are sophisticated market research techniques that have equally sophisticated names, such as *conjoint analysis*. Such techniques tend to be hard to apply, produce results that can be misleading, and, in my experience, are not that much fun.

The unfortunate result of this disparate spectrum of market research techniques is that product teams often end up engaging in sporadic or episodic customer inquiry. At times, they may ask a few customers some questions, often without a clear goal, or they may hire a specialized market research firm to apply a technique on their behalf and interpret the results. The use of outside firms increases costs, further discouraging product teams from frequently seeking the understanding of their customers that they need to generate innovations. To make matters worse, the outside firm running the study is the organization that develops the understanding, serving as an unnecessary intermediary between a company and its customers, and it is difficult to deliver the insights gained from the outside firm into the product team in a way in which the product team can act on the results. The effects of disappointing internal results and the relatively high cost of external research lead product teams to avoid market research.

Innovation Games strike a balance by moving beyond simple questions to provide you with powerful insights into customer and market needs. At the same time, they are simple and lightweight enough that you can engage them on your own. Perhaps more importantly, even when you use an outside firm to help you plan, facilitate, or post-process the results of the games, the Innovation Games process ensures that your team is the group that captures the majority of the information by having them work directly with customers.

Organizing and Using Innovation Games

There are two ways to organize Innovation Games. The first is based on the kind of understanding you seek. The second is based on the context in which you are going to apply the game.

Organizing Innovation Games

Table 1.2 organizes the games by your goals for customer understanding. Note that some games appear more than once because these games are useful in more than one context.

Table 1.2 Selecting Games that Best Meet Your Goals

What do you want to understand?	Consider These Games
Unmet and/or idealized market needs. Although all Innovation Games provide insight into market needs, these games are specifically designed for identifying unmet and/or idealized market needs, which can then be used as input to strategic planning and the identification of new business opportunities.	Product Box Me and My Shadow Buy a Feature Give Them a Hot Tub Remember the Future
Products and services usage and relationships. Successful products evolve over time, typically becoming richer and more customized to meet the needs of increasingly diverse markets. A key aspect to managing this evolution and tapping into new markets is gaining a better understanding of how customers use existing products and services and how they are related to other products and services. These games will help.	Spider Web Start Your Day Me and My Shadow Show and Tell The Apprentice
Product and service functionality. As Theodore Levitt wrote in his seminal work *The Marketing Imagination*,[1] customers don't want a drill—they want a hole. Clayton Christensen echoes this theme in *The Innovator's Dilemma*[2] by reminding us, "We hire products to do jobs." These games will help you better understand the jobs your customers are striving to accomplish.	Product Box 20/20 Vision Me and My Shadow Speed Boat Start Your Day The Apprentice Buy a Feature
How to shape your product for the future. Every company spends a lot of time thinking about the future of its products and services. Unfortunately, all too often they don't explicitly include their customers in the conversation. These games provide a way for your customer to join you in shaping your future—together.	Remember the Future 20/20 Vision Buy a Feature Prune the Product Tree

1. Levitt, T. *The Marketing Imagination*. New York, NY: The Free Press, 1986.
2. Christensen, C. M. *The Innovator's Dilemma*. Boston, MA: Harvard Business School Press, 1997.

Four Ways to Use Innovation Games

This book details four specific ways in which you can use Innovation Games. The first way is *directed market research*, or market research that is designed to answer specific questions with data that supports taking action against these data. Examples of directed market research include determining what features should be included in a specific product release or specific pain points of target markets (including, but not limited to, existing customers, prospects, competitors, channel partners, and so forth).

The second is *customer-centric innovation*, in which you use the games to uncover previously unknown market needs. As you'll see later, Innovation Games are especially effective at creating opportunities to learn "what you didn't know that you didn't know," which in many ways serves as the heart of innovation.

The third way to use Innovation Games is *generating the rich understanding of customer needs and desires* that feed the various requirements techniques we use to manage products. User personas, scenarios, and use cases, assessing feature importance through Kano analysis, or creating "nonfunctional requirements" are all important—but all come after the insights that lead to innovation, shaping them and defining them. Innovation comes before requirements, and playing Innovation Games with your customers creates richer requirements.

The fourth is *providing support and strengthening the ongoing relationship* that you have with key customers through existing channels such as customer advisory boards, user groups, and/or customer conferences. Instead of subjecting your customers to a boring afternoon of PowerPoint presentations, you can use Innovation Games to engage and energize them in a way that drives innovation.

These areas are all linked through the use of Innovation Games. For example, although you may have a specific question (directed market research), playing a game is almost certain to provide you with new information, some of which may drive innovation (customer-centric innovation). Part One starts with directed market research, because the process for using Innovation Games to support directed market research can be leveraged by the other motivations.

INNOVATION GAMES AS A MARKET RESEARCH TECHNIQUE

Because I've classified Innovation Games as a form of qualitative market research, it is appropriate to take a step back and briefly discuss the broader topic of market research. I have a sinking feeling that some of you may have cringed a bit when you read that last sentence, because not everyone has had favorable experiences with market research. It is worth making the investment to read this section because a grounding in the basics of market research is important to getting the best results from using Innovation Games, and the market research process described in this section provides a solid foundation for using the games in other contexts.

You Know Something About What You Don't Know

Individual knowledge can be organized into three areas:

- What you know
- What you don't know
- What you don't know that you don't know

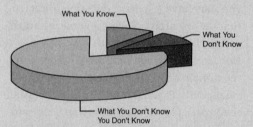

FIGURE 1.4 What You Don't Know

To illustrate: I know how to ride a bike, change a diaper, and plan, facilitate, and post process the results of an Innovation Game (and a few other things). I don't know many more things, from scuba diving to performing knee-replacement surgery.

But I can't tell you anything about what I don't know I don't know. I can't even tell you that I don't know it, because when I tell you that I don't know something, it actually means that I *do* know something—I know that I don't know it. The point is subtle and is worth repeating: When you claim that you don't know something, you actually *do* know something—you know that you don't know it. Thus, any movement from complete ignorance moves you into a continuum of knowing. We communicate our place in this continuum through convenient shorthand phrases that are contextually motivated: "Yes, I know how to play chess" or "No, I don't know how to replace the transmission on my car."

By collapsing the continuum of knowledge, we can simplify the organization of individual knowledge into two dimensions:

- What you know
- What you don't know that you don't know

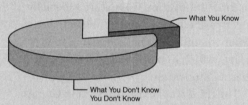

FIGURE 1.5 You Know Something About
What You Don't Know

Part of the power of Innovation Games lies in their capability to move you from complete ignorance into a state of knowing. From this state of knowing, you can choose to create a variety of innovative products and services.

As you read this, keep in mind that market research is an incredibly complex topic. This book makes no attempt at a detailed discussion of market research. I may not cover an item that you think is important. I may not cover an item you know a great deal about in sufficient depth. That's OK. My goal isn't to write the definitive reference on market research. Instead, my goal is provide enough of a foundation in market research so that you can leverage basic concepts to help you succeed whether you're a market research expert or an engineer who wants to better understand the people who are using her product.

For our purposes, it is sufficient to define market research as an ongoing process of finding answers to questions; the answers enhance your understanding of your customers, your markets, and your product and service offerings. Market research, whether sophisticated or simplistic, enables you to make better decisions with greater confidence. It is ongoing because you, your customers, and the larger product and service ecosystem in which you exist are not static.[3]

Effective market research is

- Systematic—Planned, well-organized, with a goal and a method

- Objective—Minimal researcher or method bias

- Focused—On specific questions

- Actionable—The results obtained enable you to take action

----

3. Note that this definition means that all uses of the games—even when used in requirements management—are a form of market research.

The first letter from each of these words forms the acronym SOFA, and like a comfortable SOFA, effective market research provides a comfortable position for sound decision making. As I describe the use of Innovation Games, I'll discuss how you can play them according to these tenets.

A Market Research Process

The following is an effective market research process. Although it is simple, it is not simplistic, and you'll find that using it will produce much better results than ad-hoc planning.

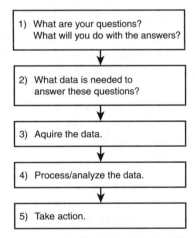

FIGURE 1.6 A Market Research Process

Step 1: Forming Questions and Preparing for Answers

The first step is determining the questions you want answered and what you will do with the answers. Both are included as part of the first step because it doesn't make much sense to ask questions if you're not committed to at least do *something* with the answers. Of course, the specific things you do, such as create new products, adjust current product road maps, or change existing products to better meet market needs, can't be predicted in advance. In this way, then, market research starts like a great vacation: you select both a destination and some activities that you'll do once you arrive, even if the activities you define in advance are as imprecise as "explore the terrain."

Step 2: Determining the Kind of Data Needed
Your questions and goals strongly determine the kind of data you'll need to acquire in your market research process, much like your vacation destination strongly influences your choice of travel. Focused and precise questions, such as "Which color of blue is most preferred by my customers," motivate the gathering of data that is very different from questions that are more open ended, such as, "How does my customer see this market landscape changing over time?"

Step 3: Acquiring the Data
This phase encompasses all the activities you need to acquire the necessary data, from planning your data acquisition method to putting it into action. Continuing with our vacation analogy, after you've selected the destination and choice of travel, you have to do the detailed planning and take the trip.

Step 4: Processing/Analyzing the Data
After you've arrived at your vacation destination, you will probably have to unpack and get ready for your activities. Similarly, after you've acquired the data, you have to process it into a form that allows people to take action. This is one of more rich and complex areas of market research, and it includes many topics that are beyond the scope of this book. Fortunately, as you'll read in Part Two, processing and analyzing game-related data is a relatively simple process.

Step 5: Taking Action
Taking action means putting your newly obtained understanding of your customers to work. In some cases, "taking action" may actually mean making no changes to your current plan, such as when you find that your product road map matches customer and market needs. In other cases, as described by Joan Waltman in her foreword, taking action may mean creating an entirely new product offering based on unexpected information, much like you might spontaneously change your vacation plans to attend a local music and arts festival that you learned about from the hotel concierge after you've checked in.

Primary and Secondary Data
Market researchers classify data according to the kinds of questions it answers. The key distinctions are *primary data*, which are data designed to answer your specific question(s) as well as possible, and *secondary data*, which are previously collected and published data that may or may not answer your specific question(s). (See Figure 1.7.) Examples of secondary data include census bureau data, which may help you broadly size your market, but may not help you determine how your customers use your product or what they might want in future products.

Primary Data designed to answer your specific question(s) as best as possible.	*Qualitative/"open ended"/"VOC":* – Focus groups – Interviews (phone, in-person) – Innovation Games – Customer advisory boards *Quantitative/"facts, choices":* – Questionnaires/Surveys
Secondary Previously collected and published data that may or may not address your specific question(s).	*Free, often under-utilized:* – Internal company records – Government data – Libraries *For sale, often market forcused:* – Syndicated or private data

FIGURE 1.7 Primary and Secondary Data Table

What Kinds of Questions?

In addition to the general destinations described in this section, you might have a whole host of specific questions regarding your products and services. Here are various questions that you might have relative to your customers, your markets, and your products and services. We'll start with secondary data, because these are the kinds of questions that are often asked when considering the broad opportunity that you're exploring through your market research.

Questions best answered through secondary data:

- Is my market growing?
- What is the median age and income of my market?
- What is the total spending on goods and services for this market?

Questions best answered through primary data:

- What kinds of products could or should we add to our product mix?
- Which color of yellow is best for our packaging?
- Which member of the family has the greatest influence in selecting products?

Questions best answered through Innovation Games:

- What features do customers want in the next release?
- How do customers use our product?
- How do my customers perceive the relationships between my product and other products?
- What is my customers' definition of success?

Primary data, on the other hand, is data acquired to answer a specific question and is further classified as qualitative and quantitative. Qualitative data is considered open ended, is usually acquired through intensive human interactions, and must be interpreted. Examples of qualitative data include focus groups, interviews, and Innovation Games. Quantitative data is based on facts or choices and can often be acquired through less intensive and/or semi-automated methods. Examples of quantitative data include surveys and conjoint analysis.

Whom Do I Ask? Market Segmentation

Primary data is acquired directly from your customers, which leads us to the process of selecting the customers who will participate in your market research. Unless your market is extremely small, you'll have to segment your market and choose representative customers from one or more of the resulting segments. Market segmentation is a process of dividing a total market into groups consisting of entities who have similar attributes that help you accomplish some larger goal, such as sales, marketing, or, in this case, better understanding customer needs.

Like other aspects of marketing, market research, and product development, market segmentation is itself a rich discipline. A market segment is just one way to slice a market, and choosing a meaningful slicing is important for your goals. A common way to segment consumers includes such things as demographic data, such as where they live,

Why Statistical Significance Doesn't Matter in Complex Business Architectures

In his seminal work on innovation, *Dealing with Darwin*, Geoffrey Moore makes a powerful case that companies who serve complex-systems markets must rely on qualitative research to guide their decisions. As Moore explains, a "Complex-systems architecture specializes in tackling complex problems and coming up with individualized solutions with a high proportion of consulting services." Such companies are characterized by relatively small numbers of customers, and a small number of transactions with each customer, with each transaction costing hundreds of thousands to millions of dollars.

As Moore describes it, qualitative scenarios drive the research efforts of complex-systems architectures. From p. 39: "In the complex-systems model, market research has a *qualitative* bias because each customer constitutes a market reality unto itself. For example, the commercial airline businesses at Airbus and Boeing have perhaps two hundred or so primary customers worldwide to consider. Statistically averaging insights across such a modest customer population makes no sense. Instead, you want to delve deeply into the specific circumstances of each account, seeking out unique patterns, not mathematical correlations. This is where war stories and hypothetical scenarios, even just the occasional apt metaphor, can prove so insightful."

Innovation Games are explicitly designed to provide you with these kinds of insights through direct interaction with your customers.

disposable income, or highest educational degrees, their purchase behavior, and their perceptions of the product and/or service being offered. Common ways to segment businesses include the kind of business, its size in terms of revenue or employees, the kind of business (corporation, sole proprietorship, LLC, and so forth), rate of growth, and markets served, to name just a few.

You may find a marketing and sales bias to your existing segmentations. This is understandable; many times the most important aspect to segmentation is helping the marketing function size the market and find leads to hand over to sales. This approach, however, may not yield the best results when considering whom to invite to an Innovation Game. Many times you'll obtain more true insights by considering alternative approaches to market segmentation. Here are some ideas to get you started:

- Experience with your product
- Knowledge of the domain
- Perceived motivation to use your product
- Strategic importance to your firm (such as by revenue)

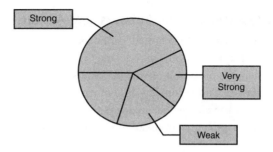

FIGURE 1.9 Knowledge of Domain

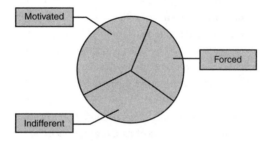

FIGURE 1.10 Perceived Motivation to Use Product

The key objective is finding the people who are most likely to provide you with the best answers to your questions. You may find that the customers who pay you the most money are not necessarily the ones who have the best handle on how your product needs to evolve to meet future needs.

After you've finished your market segmentation, you'll still need to select specific customers. This aspect of the process is covered later in Part One under the detailed notes of preparing for the game. Keep an open mind as you consider your current market segments, as playing the games may provide you with insights that motivate changing them.

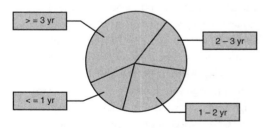

FIGURE 1.8 Experience With Product

Questions, Data, Answers, and Actions

Acquiring data is not the same as having your questions answered. One important benefit to using Innovation Games is that they can offer considerably more information: you can get the answers to your questions *and* you can make new discoveries about your market. For example, in one of the more novel applications of *Speed Boat*, I was asked to help a major law firm in Silicon Valley identify the root cause of associate dissatisfaction. In the process, we acquired data about specific issues that contributed to associate dissatisfaction—the data that

---

Whom Should I Invite? Who—or What—is a Customer?

One of the long-running debates in the field of product development is how a given product team should define a customer. When defined too narrowly, teams lose the opportunity to expand their market with new innovations or improve existing products by better understanding complex relationships. When defined too broadly or haphazardly, teams can become overwhelmed trying to make sense of data that simply does not apply to their situation. At times, emotions can get the better of common sense, with everyone—especially the customer—losing in the process. That said, it has become clear that this is an important issue and that some guidance is important.

One source of tension is that product teams struggle to capture the meaning and impact of direct and indirect customers, often at the same time. By distinguishing between these two kinds of customers, teams can gain a much richer sense of overall market needs. A *direct customer* is any person or system that directly uses or consumes your product or service. An *indirect customer* is any person or system who is or will be affected by your product or service.

The chief benefit of this definition is that it challenges you to think broadly when considering which customers you should include when considering a game. It also is practical. If you're trying to understand operational issues, deal with customers who work in operations. If you're trying to understand financial/ROI issues, get access to the people who pay the bills. If you're trying to understand the effects of slow system performance for airline reservation software, ask the airline customer who has to wait in line while the ticket agent changes his reservation. In this case, the direct customer of the software is the ticket agent, and the indirect customer is the passenger—who just happens to be the direct customer of the airline!

Don't be misled by differences in usage profiles. Some customers are power users, people who use your product or service every day. Others might be occasional or episodic users, who use your product only when motivated by certain needs or circumstances. What are those needs? Those circumstances? Different people will use different capabilities or features. Which? When? Why? All these people have a right to be heard, although you should certainly feel free to assign weights to what they've said. Although it is important to select a reasonably good set of customers to play the game you've selected, you do not have to get some "perfect" set of customers together before you can get started.

helped answer the specific question. We also acquired data far beyond the original question, such as the associates' ideas on how the law firm could better utilize IT resources and share information about the firm, all of which created new opportunities and possibilities.

Having answers to your questions does not always mean that you will take the actions it suggests. Continuing with the example of the law firm, certain actions were incongruent with the larger culture of the firm and were not taken. In terms of the vacation analogy, the law firm had a specific destination in mind and the intent to act on the data it provided. However, after they arrived at that destination, they surveyed the possibilities and chose some activities, but not others.

It is common, and often recommended, to use a combination of market research approaches to gain the confidence to take a specific course of action. Suppose that while playing *Product Box* to answer questions about marketing messages for an existing product, a customer identifies a new product opportunity. Before building this new product, you might consider engaging in other kinds of market research—for example, secondary market research to help determine the size of this market, and additional forms of primary market research to determine how much people might pay for this product.

The Unique Benefits (and Drawbacks) of Qualitative Market Research

Each form of market research has its own strengths and limitations. Table 1.3 presents some of the strengths and weaknesses of qualitative market research.

The strengths of working directly with customers through qualitative market research strongly outweigh the weaknesses. Simply put, qualitative market research (finding ways to interact, experience, and collaborate with your customers) is the strongest foundation for creating truly innovative products and services.

Table 1.3 Strengths and Weaknesses of Qualitative Market Research

Strengths	Weaknesses
Generates deeper understanding through contextual, multifaceted, verbal/nonverbal communication.	By definition, is less objective than other market research methods. We account for this in Innovation Games by using facilitators, multiple observers, and post processing results as a team.
Can strengthen customer relationships, especially in B2B and B2P markets.	Does not scale to large numbers of people.
Builds customer empathy within the team doing the research.	Is not statistically significant (see the sidebar "Why Statistical Significance Doesn't Matter in Complex Business Architectures").
Creates vivid, concrete language and commitment to solve customers problems.	Relatively costly on a "per customer" cost basis (but often relatively cheap on "actionable results" basis).
Forms the foundation of innovation by letting you explore "what you don't know you don't know."	

What Makes Innovation Games Special?

Innovation Games possess several qualities that stand out among the various approaches of qualitative market research. One quality is reflected in their name: Innovation *Games*. By referring to them as "games of collaborative play," I am intentionally conditioning your mind to think about the many fun ways you can work with your customers to better understand their needs. This can be contrasted with traditional surveys and focus groups, which are often not designed to be fun and may not include a heavy emphasis on collaboration.

The games themselves, while fun, are more than just play. As detailed in Part Two, each game leverages deep principles of cognitive psychology and organizational behavior to uncover data that is difficult to uncover using traditional market research techniques. As you come to understand the power of these deep principles, your use of the games will improve, and you'll find yourself able to discover even richer data.

One area you'll improve through experience is your willingness to put your customer in control and "trust" the process of the game. Innovation Games are not tightly controlled by a facilitator. In fact, a well-facilitated game has exactly the *opposite* effect; there is a bit of chaotic fun as customers become fully engaged in the game. You'll know a game is going really well when your customers don't want to stop playing (drawing their spider webs or creating their product boxes, for instance). This is precisely what you want, for when customers are fully engaged in the task, they won't want to stop. Neither will you, because it is this deep level of engagement that gets past any barriers to communication and produces the most honest and useful feedback.

Innovation Games are also distinguished from other forms of market research that do not involve the product team in the preparation phase and leave the product team as distant observers during the research. In an Innovation Game, the team is expected to actively participate in preparing for the game (and have fun doing so). During the game, even one that is professionally facilitated by a third party, a cross-functional product team is expected to act as observers who are involved firsthand in gathering data from customers. They see product boxes being created and hear them being sold. They watch product trees take shape and listen to customers explain how they are growing over time. They see complex spider webs of relationships emerge and can explore why these relationships are important to customers. This can be contrasted to other forms of qualitative research in which teams are hidden behind a two-way mirror or are looking through the small lens of a video camera.

Preparing to play the games helps product teams confirm their goals for their offerings and their goals for the market research. Playing the games internally before playing the games with customers helps increase your confidence in the power of the games. This doesn't mean that the games are complex. Quite the contrary. The games are designed to be simple to explain, simple to play, and rich in results.

All the games are designed to leverage multiple dimensions of communication because multidimensional communication enables us to access the full power of our brain. To illustrate, a traditional survey or focus group mostly leverages the language-processing centers of our brain. Although clearly important, language is only one dimension of communication. Innovation Games let customers engage other centers of their brain, resulting in richer, deeper, and more meaningful exchanges of information. Examples of this rich communication range from the spatial arrangement of anchors when playing *Speed Boat* to the way customers react to each other when sharing their use of a product in *Start Your Day*. The richness of these communications find their way back into the organization through the often stunning commitment to action that results from Innovation Games. The experience of reading about a desired new product feature written in a Marketing Requirements Document is radically different than the experience of seeing this same feature described on a product box generated by a customer.

I've experienced the same level of commitment from customers who play Innovation Games. Many of the games are based on customers working together creating, negotiating, explaining, prioritizing, and envisioning the products and services that will enable them to accomplish their goals. By giving them a shared voice, Innovation Games not only improve relationships between you and your customers, it encourages them to create and sustain relationships among each other. Although this may not be reflected directly in your cash flow statement, consider that your balance sheet does have a line item for Good Will. Playing the games will increase it.

An additional benefit of Innovation Games is that instead of producing a dry report of your analysis and recommendations, you can bring back the various artifacts created by customers. As one Director of Product Marketing described it, instead of endlessly debating the "perfect" marketing messages to promote a new product, she simply pointed out the surprising commonality of the common marketing slogans coined by several customers playing *Product Box* and said: "Our customers wrote this. We're going to use it." By leveraging direct customer feedback, she saved considerable time and expense.

THE INNOVATION GAMES PROCESS

The process for playing Innovation Games is based on the market research process described earlier. Most of the steps are the same, but there are a few twists that we'll cover in this section (see Figure 1.11). Part Three of this book includes tools and templates that you can use to help guide you through this process.

Step 1: Forming Questions and Preparing for Answers

As a form of qualitative market research, Innovation Games are useful in answering many of your questions, but certainly not all of them. The key step here is making sure your goals and questions are appropriate for Innovation Games. This is so important that I've devoted the next section to this topic. It is also important to emphasize that you shouldn't play a game unless you're committed to taking some kind of action based on the results. Innovation Games tend to increase expectations among your customers that you will be doing something with their feedback.

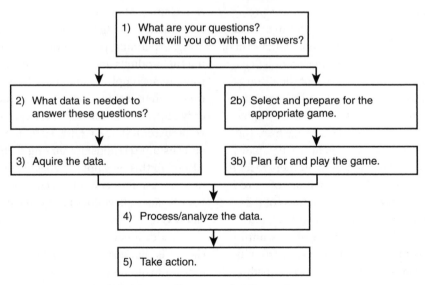

FIGURE 1.11 The Innovation Games Process

Respond in the Report, Not in Real-time

The collaborative nature of Innovation Games gives you plenty of opportunity to respond to customer feedback in real-time. For example, *Speed Boat* explicitly asks customers to tell you what they don't like about your product or service, and many times customers will try and pin you down for a specific time frame for fixing a perceived problem. Similarly, *Buy a Feature* asks customers to collaborate on purchasing their most desired features. When done, they may ask you for commitments on when you'll be delivering on the features they've purchased.

Do everything in your power to resist responding to customer requests in real-time. Responding to requests substantially changes, and can unintentionally stop, the flow of information from your customers. Instead of gathering data, you're responding to problems. They'll realize this, and the most vocal customers will take charge to try and get what they want.

And what your most vocal customers want may not be what the rest of your customers want. You need time to think through the data you obtain while playing the game before committing to a plan of action.

Indeed, committing to a plan of action is risky, as making commitments to customers during a game is almost certainly going to circumvent your normal planning processes. In one situation I've seen these normal planning processes overturn, for good reasons, a commitment made during a game. Explaining this to the affected customers was not fun.

After you have committed to a plan of action, you will want to share this with all your customers. For the customers who played the game, you'll want to share your plan of action in a way that emphasizes how their feedback helped to create this plan. For example, if their feedback resulted in modifications to a development road map, show them the old road map along with the new road map so they can trace the effects of their participation in the games. For your other customers, you'll want to leverage your normal communication channels to keep them up to date on your plans.

Step 2: Determining the Kind of Data Needed

This step of the market research process is now focused on selecting the right set of games to accomplish the goals and answer the question you've identified in step 1.

Step 3: Acquiring the Data

This phase encompasses planning and playing the game. This is also discussed in greater detail later in Part One; you'll get the best results if you follow a detailed planning sequence and play the games with a structured team.

Step 4: Processing/Analyzing the Data

There are two audiences for the results that you'll produce from processing and analyzing the data that you obtain during the game. The first is your internal team, and the result[4] you produce for them should contain

---

4. The result you produce could be a report, a presentation, a debriefing meeting with senior executives, or a set of specific recommendations loaded into your requirements management or Product Lifecycle Management (PLM) system. You should choose the format that is most likely to motivate your team to take action.

whatever is needed to take action. The second is the customers who played the game. Creating a result for them (typically a report) lets them know that you've heard what they had to say. It also gives you a chance to respond to their feedback in a controlled manner, when you've had a chance to think through the implications of your response and to tailor your response to meet the needs of specific customers. For example, during a recent game of *Speed Boat*, a customer wrote "Price discounts are confusing." Apparently, this was the only customer who felt this way, because none of the other customers playing the game felt that the price discounts were confusing. Still, this was valuable feedback, and the report mailed to this specific customer included additional information on product pricing.

Step 5: Taking Action

This is the step in which Innovation Games are most like other forms of market research. The goal of playing the games is to always take action with the results.

SELECTING THE RIGHT INNOVATION GAME

As you become comfortable with playing Innovation Games, you'll find that it is rather easy to start with a high-level goal and then select the game that will help you best accomplish this goal. For example, suppose that you'd like to involve your customers in creating your product road map. Using Table 1.2 and the cards in the back of the book, you've narrowed down your choice to *Buy a Feature* and *Prune the Product Tree*. In fact,

they both sound so good that you'd like to play them both, but you don't have enough time for this. You have to pick one. To help you make your choice, this section characterizes the various games along several key dimensions. Be careful about making your choice solely on reading this section, however, because each of the games can be tailored. The detailed descriptions of the games in Part Two will help you make your final choice, along with showing you how you can tailor the games to meet your circumstances. Here are the six dimensions that this section explores:

- Degree of open-ended exploration
- Number of customers who can play the game
- Three aspects of preparation: Physical, Market, and Customer
- Time frame of action

To help reinforce the idea that these are somewhat loose characterizations, the games are drawn in gauge format. These gauges will be repeated with each innovation game in Part Two for easy reference.

Degree of Open-Ended Exploration

The degree of open-ended exploration refers to how much—or how little—you constrain interaction with a customer (see Figure 1.12). For example, *Buy a Feature* is one of the more constrained games because customers are working together to purchase the features that you've already priced. In contrast, *Speed Boat* and *Product Box* are both very unconstrained. In *Speed Boat*, customers can (and do!) write down just about anything on an anchor card. In *Product Box*, you're giving

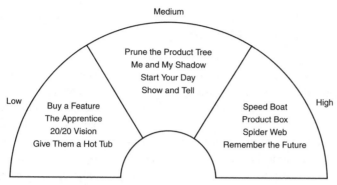

FIGURE 1.12 Degree of Open-Ended Exploration

the customer a blank box and literally asking them to draw whatever they'd like. These unconstrained interactions tend to produce very open-ended explorations.

Many games enable you to vary the degree of exploration. For example, you can make *Me and My Shadow* more open ended by shadowing customers as they perform general tasks, both with and without your products and services. Alternatively, you can constrain *Me and My Shadow* to focus primarily or solely on a predefined set of tasks or just your products and services. Let the questions that are motivating your use of the games inform the degree of open-ended exploration you'll bring to the game.

Number of Customers Who Can Play the Game

Innovation Games are designed for relatively small groups, typically between 4 and 24 people. However, we have had success in scaling some of the games to several hundred people. (See Figure 1.13.) The two key tricks in scaling the games to large groups is leveraging the natural structure of the games to

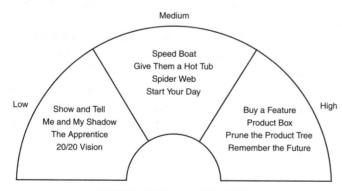

FIGURE 1.13 Degree of Scalability

subdivide larger groups into smaller groups that can play the games and changing the degree of facilitation within the games.

There is a limit to this process, however, no matter what game you're playing. For example, *20/20 Vision* is a game that works best with a facilitator managing the discussion between 6 to 12 customers. If you want more customers to participate, you're going to need more facilitators, which naturally limits the degree of scalability. Also, keep in mind that larger groups produce more results, increasing both the complexity and time required to effectively post process these results into an agreed upon plan of action.

Preparation Workload

There are three dimensions of preparation work for an Innovation Game: physical/materials preparation, market preparation, and customer preparation.

Degree of Physical Preparation

The degree of physical preparation addresses the various supplies or materials that you need to play a game (see Figure 1.14). Games such as *Remember the Future* or *20/20 Vision*, which require nothing more than standard flip charts or 5"×8" index cards, have a low degree of physical preparation, whereas others, such as *Product Box*, which requires a relatively large set of office supplies, have higher physical preparation requirements.

Degree of Market Preparation

The degree of market preparation concerns how much effort you have to put into preparing the content for the game (see Figure 1.15). *Product Box* ranks quite low in this dimension, because in *Product Box* you're not asking your customers to respond to your ideas. In contrast, *20/20 Vision* ranks higher because you have to take the time to prepare the items (content) you want your customers to prioritize. Keep in mind that games that require more market preparation often help product teams make valuable choices—even before playing the games with their customers!

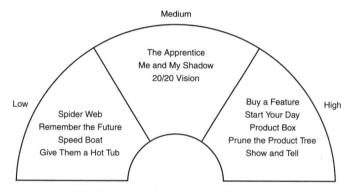

FIGURE 1.14 Degree of Physical Preparation

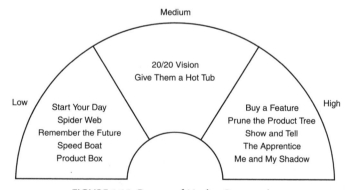

FIGURE 1.15 Degree of Market Preparation

Degree of Customer Preparation

The degree of customer preparation concerns how much effort your customers will have to put into preparing to play the game. Both *Product Box* and *20/20 Vision* rank low in this regard because in these games you're looking for the real-time reactions of customers during the game. In contrast, *Show and Tell* ranks much higher because you're explicitly asking customers to tell you about how they use your products and services. (See Figure 1.16.) Your customers who will be participating in the game will need time to prepare for this.

Time Frame of Action

The games also vary by the time frame for putting the result of the game into action. Classifying time frames is very challenging because product cycle times differ so much by industries. Instead of giving you absolutes, I'll instead classify the time frame for action in terms of cycle times, with the understanding that each of the games has the potential to produce results that can span a wide range of times for action. (See Figure 1.17.)

- Shorter/Tactical—Actions that can be taken right away, typically in the current or next product cycle.

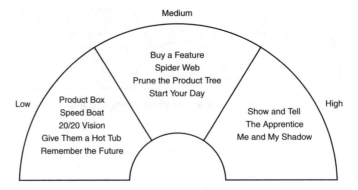

FIGURE 1.16 Degree of Customer Preparation

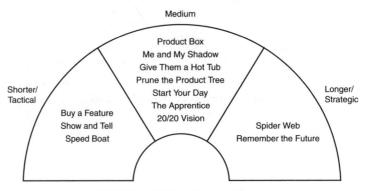

FIGURE 1.17 Time Frame of Action

- Medium—Actions that are typically taken in the next one to three product cycles.
- Longer/Strategic—Actions that are typically taken over the course of many product cycles.

Keep in mind that a combination of factors helps regulate customers' expectations about the time frame of action. If you're playing *Buy a Feature*, it is typically because you want feedback about the next one or two product releases. Similarly, if you're playing *Remember the Future*, in which the future is 10 years from now, customers will readily expect that the time frame of action will be longer. Many customers, especially in business and professional markets, have a reasonable sense of the time frame associated with a suggested or requested action. They may even expect that something will take a longer time to accomplish based on their own strategic and tactical planning cycles. Keep in mind that you can always check your understanding of how quickly your customers expect you to act: just ask them.

If You Feel Overwhelmed by 12 Choices

During one class I was teaching on Innovation Games, the Senior Director of Product Management pulled me aside and said, "Twelve choices feels like too many. I know all of the games are good, but can you pick just a few that address universal themes and are relatively easy to play? This would help my team get started in using these games that much faster." Here is the list that I gave him:

Speed Boat Even the most satisfied customers have ideas on how you can improve your products and services. *Speed Boat* gives your customers an opportunity to share these ideas with you.

Buy a Feature Product development is a constant art of managing to deliver the most important features within limited resources. To make this even more challenging, most product teams have more ideas on what features they should add to their products than the resources needed to add them. *Buy a Feature* helps you make tough prioritization decisions by giving your customers a voice in the prioritization process.

Product Box Good product managers have a strong point of view about what their market needs. Great product managers take the time to explore "what they don't know they don't know" through open-ended, qualitative market research. *Product Box* provides you with new possibilities through open-ended exploration.

Spider Web You need to understand how your product fits into your customers' world so that you can make effective choices about what does and does not go into your product. By asking your customers to explain their view of how your product fits into their world, *Spider Web* can help you do this.

Planning Your Innovation Game

Planning your game consists of two parts: a high-level event planning process that is suitable for every game and a game-specific planning process that is unique to each game. This section addresses the high-level event planning process from two perspectives: your customer's and your internal team's. Part Two addresses game-specific planning processes in the detailed description of each game. I won't try to cover every aspect of game or event planning, because planning a successful Innovation Game is a lot like planning other events, and you can easily find resources on the Internet to help you in planning events. Instead, I'll try to focus on the most essential game-related aspects of a successful event.

Before reading this section, read the sidebar "Using *Innovation Games* to Plan Your Innovation Game" to plan your event. By using the Innovation Game *Remember the Future* to help plan your event, you will create a more effective event and you will gain comfort in using Innovation Games.

A Planning Timeline

The easiest way to plan your Innovation Game is to leverage the market research process described earlier by organizing the phases into a timeline, as shown in Figure 1.18. It is helpful to further break down the high-level phases into sub-phases because there is a natural progression to each phase.

Using *Innovation Games* to Plan Your Innovation Game

You can use several Innovation Games to help you plan your event. *20/20 Vision* can help you prioritize your goals for the event, and *Speed Boat* can help you identify how to improve the results of previous events. But the game I find most useful is *Remember the Future*.

Start by opening a blank document in your favorite word processor. Imagine that it is one week *after* your event. Now, write yourself a letter from your boss, congratulating you on a remarkably successful Innovation Game event.

Be as specific as possible in the details associated with the event you will have had.

When finished, compare the results of your letter with the advice in this section. You'll probably find that you identified many of the activities covered in this section. More importantly, you're also likely to find some key items that are unique to your situation. In either case, you've played the Innovation Game *Remember the Future*, and in the process you've learned a powerful technique that can help you plan all kinds of projects.

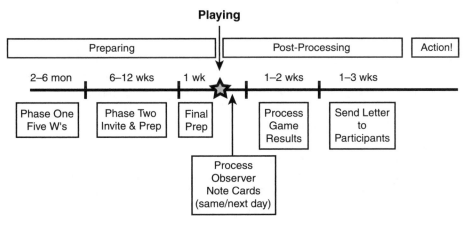

FIGURE 1.18 A Timeline for Planning and Playing an Innovation Game

Phases of Preparation

It is most convenient to prepare for Innovation Games in phases based on the lead time and activities associated with each phase. For example, determining whom to invite, securing the meeting place, and selecting the game can all take a fair amount of time, so they are included in phase one. Inviting customers and performing all preparation work is part of phase two. Final preparations include double-checking all supplies and making sure your team is ready. The remainder of this section reviews the activities of each phase in greater detail.

Phase One: The Five W's

The "Five W's" is project planning shorthand for the phase of the project that answers basic logistics and operational questions associated with the event. Answering them enables you and your customers to do everything from packing the right clothing to determining whether they might want to

bring their partners or families to the event for any social or fun activities that you may have planned. This section covers just the "Five W's," and if you're an experienced event planner, this may be all that you need in this phase of planning your Innovation Game. Additional phase one planning activities are included in Part Three. And yes, for those of you who are keeping track, I've included more than five questions—on purpose!

- **Whom** are you inviting? Consider customers and your internal project team both. A good rule of thumb is between 12 and 36 customers; research has shown that 12 customers are expected to represent 70 to 75 percent of market needs, and 30 customers can be expected to represent 90 percent of market needs.[5]

---

5. Griffin, Abbie and John R. Hauser: "The Voice of The Customer" in Marketing Science, Vol. 12, No. 1, Winter 1993, pp. 1–27.

Customer Benefits

The top three customer benefits from playing an Innovation Game are

- An opportunity to strongly influence current and future products.

- An opportunity to meet and build relationships with other customers.

- An opportunity to meet and interact with the product team, including the senior executives who are often present at such events.

Customers also get game-specific benefits depending on the game being played and/or the structure of the event. Examples of these kinds of benefits include

- Exclusive insight into key features planned for future product releases and the ability to influence and change them.

- An opportunity to share current pain points.

- A way to make money or win some prizes.

- **What** will you be doing? Consider both the games and related event activities.

- **Why** are you doing these things? **Why** should your customer come? Consider your customer understanding and customer relationship goals and explicitly show them "What's In It for Them."

- **When** is the event?

- **How long** is the event? A safe estimate is two hours per game, with no more than three games in one day. Add additional time to handle your other event goals.

- **Where** is the event?

- **What** happens at the end of the event? Customers will want to know what they receive as a result of participating in the event. If you're going to send them a summary of what you learned (and you should), tell them.

Phase Two: Invite and Prep

In this phase of the planning process, you'll be communicating the key details of the event to your customers and finalizing all the logistics. Strive to keep an external, customer-centric focus on the information you share with your customers. They have questions, and while you should have answered all of them in your phase one planning process, you need to communicate this information in a direct, respectful, and straightforward manner. Part Three contains sample invitation letters that you can tailor to meet your needs.

I've found the following checklist helpful during phase two of the planning process:

❑ Appropriate food has been ordered.

❑ All equipment (A/V) is ready.

❑ We have practiced playing the game.

❏ All speakers have rehearsed their presentations.

❏ The room is properly configured per the specific game requirements.

❏ The team has been briefed on their roles.

❏ All graphics and game-specific materials have been created. Be especially careful to give yourself enough time for preparation-intensive games such as *Product Box* or *Prune the Product Tree.*

❏ All gifts and/or other materials have been delivered and are ready for distribution.

❏ Event evaluation forms have been prepared.

This checklist isn't designed for every conceivable planning scenario, so you need to "check the checklist" to make certain you're covering all your needs. If you're new to event planning, consider hiring an event planning service. There are many great event planning services, and you should be able to find one that meets your needs. You should also check the Internet, as there are many useful checklists available for different event planning situations.

Final Preparation

Here is where you give yourself a chance to triple-check that everything is ready—and give yourself the chance to make a late night run to Kinko's or Walgreen's if something is missing! Refer to the "generic materials checklist" in Part Three to make certain you have all the basic materials that you need. The most important aspect of the final preparation phase is having someone on your team personally contact the participants to confirm their attendance. Use this information to plan your final seating arrangements, confirm your food purchases, and organize any materials you will be creating and/or giving to participants.

ORGANIZING YOUR TEAM

Conducting an Innovation Game is too much work for one person. You need a team organized around the following roles:

- A planner who plans for and prepares your team for the games.

- An organizer who handles logistics.

- A greeter or master of ceremonies who greets customers and invites them to the game.

- A facilitator who runs the event.

- A helper who acts as the "go-fer" for the team.

- Several observers who observe participants as they play the games.

- A photographer to record the event.

A well-sized team should be one-third to one-half the size of the customer participant team. Each role is essential to the success of the game and will be discussed in greater detail.

Planner

The planner, typically a product or marketing manager, is the project manager for the event. Starting with the market research process presented earlier, they are responsible for ensuring that everything runs smoothly. How this happens varies considerably and depends on many factors unique to your company and its corporate culture.

One area of difference concerns the degree of internal collaboration required to manage the project. In some companies the planner will follow the market research process without much input from other people. In other companies, the first step of the planner is to organize a cross-functional team who will work together to define the goals and/or questions of the market research and how the organization intends to act on the results. Both approaches work fine. Innovation Games and the process for using them should be leveraged in the context of your existing project management structures, not as a replacement.

Other areas of responsibility for the planner include making certain everyone on the team is prepared for the game. This means that each member of the team knows his or her role and the responsibilities associated with that role, with a special emphasis on observers, because observers are the people most likely to unintentionally cause problems during an Innovation Game by trying to participate or control the process.

The responsibility extends to the customers who will play the games. The planner is responsible for making certain that invitations are sent to customers that frame the right set of expectations for participation. Part Three contains templates and sample letters for planners.

The planner may have additional responsibilities ranging from formalizing the budget for the games, selecting whom to invite, making decisions about any gifts given to attendees, and so forth.

Organizer

The organizer manages the logistics of the event, including, but not limited to, the following:

- Securing an appropriate location
- Purchasing food
- Acquiring and preparing materials
- Inviting and keeping track of participants
- Preparing place cards[6] and coordinating itineraries
- Helping to collect results after the games are finished
- Managing the real-time logistics

The organizer has a big job, and if you've never done it before you may want to consider hiring an outside event planning service to help you make certain things go smoothly.

Greeter

The greeter (or master of ceremonies) welcomes participants, inviting them into the event and establishing a warm rapport. It is often a good idea to have the project manager who presides over the subject area explored by the game be the greeter. The advantage to this approach is that the greeter can leverage an existing relationship with customers who are playing the game. A key disadvantage is that it is hard for the greeter to be an observer because the greeter has varying responsibilities throughout the

---

6. Place cards are an elegant way to control seating. See Part Three for more information on how to use place cards.

playing of the game. As a result, product managers who are greeters may find that they miss a lot of what's happening during the playing of the game. Although very few of the roles can be shared, the planner and greeter can be the same person.

Facilitator

The facilitator manages the playing of the game. They have the following responsibilities:

- The facilitator explains the games being played, describing their use and answering questions from participants. To maintain consistency, it is best if the facilitator is the only person answering questions. In describing the games, the facilitator should emphasize that the primary purpose of the games is to better understand customers. As such, there are no right or wrong answers.

- The facilitator controls the pacing and tempo of the game. While never rushed or hurried, the facilitator may pick up the pace when group interest starts to wane or allow things to progress more slowly if a lot of information is being shared.

- The facilitator monitors participation levels. For example, if a relatively quiet customer is nodding her head in agreement but not speaking very much, the facilitator might ask her to state her point of view on a topic. Similarly, the facilitator will encourage customers to provide feedback and questions directly to other customers.

- The facilitator manages time. This isn't the same thing as rigidly adhering to a predetermined schedule. Instead, it is making certain that everyone is aware of, and agrees to, the overall timing of the event.

The most important responsibility for the facilitator is to manage the game so that the outcomes created are most likely to answer the goals that motivated the playing of the game in the first place. In service of this highest-level goal, the facilitator is given complete authority over everyone. Using this authority properly often means that the facilitator must be fearless when interacting with participants and managing the customer team. By fearless, I mean that the facilitator must be willing to ask tough questions of participants. At the same time, the facilitator may have to go so far as to ask observers to leave the room if their presence or behavior hinders the game. For these reasons it is often advisable to hire a third party or use someone who is not intimately associated with your product as your facilitator.

Helper

A helper is the "go-fer" for the facilitator, so named because he or she is ready, willing, and able to help with anything that might be needed. I've used helpers to do such things as making certain customers playing *Product Box* have all the materials they need to collecting and taping *Speed Boat* anchor cards to the walls.

Benefits to Using a Professional Facilitator

The Qualitative Research Consultants Association provides a comprehensive set of reasons why you should consider hiring a professional facilitator trained in market research. From their web site, www.qcra.org, these reasons go beyond the facilitation I describe in this book to include additional skills you are likely to find valuable when playing your game.

A professional knows how to

- Establish rapport with respondents
- Probe beyond rationalizations to uncover genuine motivations
- Interpret and build on what he or she hears
- Maintain flexibility in guiding the discussion without losing sight of the objectives
- "Turn on a dime"—adapt the approach when the professional and the clients encounter unexpected issues or insights
- Manage the energy level and personality dynamics of the discussion
- Avoid creating bias among respondents

A professional is prepared for challenging situations and is able to

- Get around respondents' defensive behavior
- Effectively handle talkers and nontalkers
- Keep unexpected issues from sabotaging the discussion
- Notice contradictions that don't "ring true"
- Handle sensitive topics with diplomacy
- Recognize problem respondents and act appropriately

A professional brings

- Mastery of multiple techniques
- Experience in diverse disciplines
- Knowledge about relevant trends in other categories and industries

A professional does more than moderate. A professional also

- Helps sharpen the focus and clarify the objectives of the research
- Ensures objectivity from the design stage through final analysis
- Stays focused on clients' business issues to ensure that the research findings are relevant and actionable
- Builds a positive working relationship with clients
- Helps keep the research team objective about the topic
- Stands up to pressure when necessary based on the research learning

A professional ensures high standards by

- Protecting client confidentiality
- Protecting respondent confidentiality and anonymity[7]
- Staying committed to nondiscriminatory recruiting
- Being considerate and respectful of respondents and their differences

Enthiosys maintains a network of certified facilitators to help you plan, play, and post process the results of your game.

---

7. This is not applicable when playing Innovation Games, as game participants will come to know each other through the playing of the games.

Observers

Observers watch participants as they play the games, recording their observations on 5"×8" cards. These cards will be collected and processed after the game. It works best if observers remain close enough to participants to overhear their shared conversations, but far enough to let participants speak privately if they so desire. Observers should refrain from speaking directly with participants.

Observers should write down anything that they think is important. It is really that simple. The goal isn't to write down only the most "important" or "meaningful" observation. In fact, striving to capture the "perfect" observation means that you're going to miss most of what is going on, because your brain is no longer observing, but trying to draw meaningful conclusions. Instead, the goal is to capture a lot of observations and then use the post-processing phase of the game to sort out the meaning of these observations.

Observations can include such things as

- Statements about products or services:

  Example: "Sarah said our flip-shifter doesn't connect with the mega-cranzer."

  Example: "Ramesh wondered why we don't offer integrated training—he said he'd pay for it."

- Reactions of participants about the topics that have been discussed:

  Example: "No one seemed to agree with Ramesh. Should training be included?"

  Example: "Lots of customers need special end-of-month reporting."

Observer Note Cards

To help observers remember that their job is to observe, I like to print special 5"×8" cards with observer instructions that I put inside the stack of blank cards given to observers.

> Observe the speaker.
> Observe how others are responding to the speaker.
> Write one observation per card.
> Can you capture at least 25 observations?
> Who will capture the most observations?

FIGURE 1.19 Observer Note Cards

- Things that surprised them:

  Example: "Why didn't anyone point out our online training videos?"

  Example: "Ming got our prices all wrong—how could that be?"

- Things that seemed to generate a lot of discussion:

  Example: "Lots of discussion about a potential partnership with Acme."

  Example: "Need to explore more about distribution channels."

Observers are typically drawn from the product team. It is best if your observers represent different disciplines, such as engineering, design, development, manufacturing, sales, customer service, distribution, and so forth. More observers are better, provided you don't overwhelm your customers—5 customers and 20 observers is not a recipe for success. A better ratio of observers to customers is between one-third and one-half of the total number of customers. Thus, if you have 18 customers, you'll want between 6 and 9 observers.

You need to consider the benefits and drawbacks of associating observers with customers with whom they have personal relationships (such as in sales or marketing relationships). Some of the benefits include

Chances Are the Team Will Talk

Although I recommend that only the facilitator speak with customers during the games, chances are good that observers and other members of the team will talk with customers. Many times this can be a positive experience, such as when an observer asks questions that allows the team to better explore and/or understand what a participant is saying. Allowing observers to speak, however, does carry some risks, which can be mitigated through the following guidelines:

- Avoid making any promises on anything that you cannot directly control.

- Avoid commitments to specific features or deliverables.

- Never talk negatively about your product or your competitor's products. If a customer is expressing a complaint or a concern, listen—don't commiserate.

- Refrain from asking your customers how they would solve a problem. Your focus should be on developing understanding and identifying needs, not asking for their solutions.

- If customers offer a solution, simply thank them.

- Never say, "That should be easy." It sets expectations too high and can kill any negotiation opportunities.

- Never say, "That is too hard." It can prematurely stop conversation about what the customer really wants and ways to achieve this. Besides, solving hard problems is fun and typically more profitable.

- Listen nonjudgmentally. They are your customers. They're not stupid. They're not lazy.

the natural rapport and comfort that exists and the ability to better convey some of the deeper motivations of the customers' behaviors during the game. One of the drawbacks is that familiarity often lulls observers into a false sense of confidence. They become lazy in recording their observations because they're sure they know how their customers will respond and fail to capture when customers don't act according to their preconceived ideas. A related negative behavior is when an observer forces a customer's response to fit their preexisting ideas.

It is essential that observers *do not* use laptops, PDAs, or cell phones unless it is a genuine emergency. Using these devices during a game is rude and disrespectful to your customers.

Photographer

Perhaps my favorite role is what we jokingly refer to as the "Bad Wedding Photographer." The purpose of the "Bad Wedding Photographer" is to take lots and lots of pictures of the event with a high-resolution digital camera to help in processing the results and motivating others to take action based on customer feedback. In fact, many times people who have used Innovation Games have commented that the event photos were simply invaluable in helping others understand what customers did during the event.

We refer to this person as the "Bad Wedding Photographer" because we want to eradicate the notion that you should have a small number of highly posed or otherwise professionally created photos. Posing or posturing for a photographer will inhibit the free flow of information that is essential

in an Innovation Game. You'll get the best results if you try to take so many photos that customers forget that a photographer is present. A good target is 200 photos. You almost certainly won't take that many, but *trying* to take that many will help customers feel comfortable with the person taking photos.

The Day of Your Innovation Game

The day of the actual event is where all of your preparation comes together. Although it is common to have some surprises, good preparation makes for a good game. The remainder of this section provides some general tips and techniques for playing the games. The detailed information on how to play each game is the subject of Part Two. Part Three contains detailed information that helps you plan the detailed agenda, including how much time you should allocate for the activities that often go along with the game.

- Arrive at least two hours early, and earlier if you're playing a game that requires a lot of setup. Many of the games can require several hours to set up. I've played versions of *Product Box* and *Prune the Product Tree* that have taken four to five people three to four hours to set up. In the first photo sequence, we started with a traditionally prepared meeting room, and several hours later had it organized for *Product Box*. In the second photo sequence, we started with an empty conference room and organized for *Prune the Product Tree* to be played over lunch, working side by side with the hotel wait staff. Give yourself plenty of time.

FIGURE 1.20 Setting Up for the Product Box Innovation Game

FIGURE 1.21 Setting Up for the Prune the Product Tree Innovation Game

- Have a plan for what you should do with customers if they arrive early. Some options include letting them do other work, giving them demos of products or simply engaging them in small talk. Avoid starting your game until you have all of the customers you want.

- Have a contingency plan in case a large number of your customers arrive late. In this case you might want to begin playing your originally planned game with the smaller number of customers so that you can manage your time. Although this can make it awkward for customers who arrive late to join the game, you'll still have the opportunity to get as much information as possible.

- It is helpful to share contact information. An elegant way to do this is to purchase a business card holder and preload it with the business cards of your team.

- Although I've rarely had a problem with customers using laptops, PDAs, and/or cell phones in an inappropriate manner, you may want to communicate your policy to attendees.

Processing the Results of Your Innovation Game

The primary goal of processing the results is to transform what your customers did and all that your team observed into a useful action plan. Following are four key steps in this phase:

1. Capture and process all customer artwork.

2. Capture and process all observer cards.

3. Conduct a brief retrospective of the event so that you can improve it for the next time.

4. Prepare two reports: an internal report that details the actions you will take and an external report provided to customers, letting them know what you've learned.

A common mistake in this phase is to underestimate the time required to process game results. One team we worked with had allocated only 8 person-hours (2 people for four hours) to process the result. They needed more than 80! A better rule is to allocate roughly 40 person-hours per game.

Step One: Process Customer Artwork

Customer artwork refers to the various artifacts that customers create while playing an Innovation Game. These range from simple easel paper or 5"×8" cards taped to walls to product boxes describing their ideal product. This section covers the basics, and Part Two details how to process the results of each game.

The most important guideline is to photograph everything generated by customers so that you will have a direct and permanent record of the artwork. Photos should be taken immediately after finishing the game to minimize the risk that something will be accidentally thrown out by an overly eager cleaning crew. These photographs augment and enhance the photographs created by the "Bad Wedding Photographer" during the event. These photographs should be taken with relative care because you will be using them during post processing activities and for sharing with your internal team. You may also share some of these with the customers who participated in the game, so they should be as high quality as you can make them, including using image-editing software to enhance the images.

Some of the games generate results that should be shared directly with product teams. For example, *Show and Tell, Product Box, Spider Web,* and *Start Your Day* are all games that create artwork that should be directly shared with product teams. Instead of telling them about what customers did in your final report, you can *show* them what customers created. Doing so fosters a strong incentive to act on the information generated by your customer.

Step Two: Process Observer Cards

During the game, observers were writing down their observations, ideally one observation per card. In this phase of the processing, you'll mine these observations for actionable patterns. The process is relatively simple and should be done as quickly as possible after the event, with all observers present. It is helpful if the facilitator or planner leads this process, because it allows the observers to concentrate on sharing and explaining their observations.

1. Review each card to make certain it contains one distinct observation. If a card contains multiple observations, create new cards for each observation, adhering to the guideline of one observation per card.

2. Tape all cards on the wall.

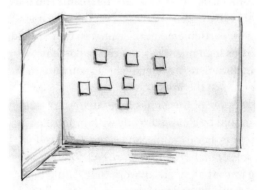

FIGURE 1.22 Place the Observer Cards on the Wall

3. Have all the observers review the cards, organizing them into groups as they deem appropriate.

4. A card can be placed into multiple groups—just create a copy of the card and place it into both groups.

5. You'll often find that several observers captured the same comment. When facilitating, I like to keep each individual card, whereas other facilitators put a number on the card indicating the number of observers who captured the same comment and dispose of the duplicates. Either way works just fine.

FIGURE 1.23 Organize the Cards into Groups as Needed

6. As groups of cards solidify, create a special card that captures the important concept that unifies the cards within that group. For example, suppose that when playing *Start Your Day* several observers noted that customers use your product very differently in the fall than in the spring, summer, or winter. You might create a group heading card called "Fall" and organize cards under this heading.

7. Keep this process going until observers stop moving cards around and there are no more groupings. Some observations may not fall into any group—that is okay. Not every card has to be put into a group.

Pause here and photograph the results. This will ensure that you have a record of the observer comments in the base categories that they created. After you've got everything photographed, keep going.

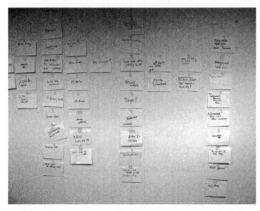

FIGURE 1.24 The Final Observer Note Cards

The facilitator and/or planner hands each observer an index card and asks the observers to quietly write down the top three things that they observed during the game. The facilitator then collects these and reviews them with the entire team. Quite often, the top three items will have surprising similarities among observers. In one event, five observers all identified the same items.

The facilitator should make one final pass over all the observations, making certain they understand each of the groupings as well as all the individual observations. The observations are then coded into a spreadsheet under the groupings described earlier for easy reference, searching, and sharing. It is not important to record which observer generated what observation.

Step Three: Retrospective

A brief retrospective of the event should be held, ideally when the entire team is present. Although there are many ways to conduct a retrospective, a simple format consisting of the following questions is usually sufficient:

- What worked so well that we should do it again?

- What worked so badly that we should never do it again?

- What should we try changing?

Step Four: Prepare Reports

There are two reports that must be prepared. They are equally important, for different reasons. The first report is designed for internal distribution. A simple organization, such as that defined in Table 1.4, works well. The focus is on the action you intend to take and the necessary information obtained during the event that supports this action. The second report will be distributed to customers who attended the event. You should prepare the internal report first, because it almost always contains elements that you will want to include in your external report. Table 1.4 captures the critical elements of the internal report.

Table 1.4 Critical Elements of an Internal Report

Section	Contents
Executive Summary	Recap of the motivations and goals of the project and the key learnings and recommended actions. Typically this is 1 to 3 pages. A few well-placed photos can do wonders.
Results for Each Game	Overview of each game played and the key results of each as described in Part Two. More photos of the event are useful here.
Retrospective Results	The summarized results of the retrospective.

The primary purpose of the customer report is to let your customers know that you heard them, that you value their input, and that you will take action on the data acquired. The customer report can be as simple as a one-page summary or as elaborate as a detailed action plan that captures the results of the feedback. Timeliness is essential, and you'll find your customers would prefer a short report distributed within two weeks of the event to a longer report distributed four months later. If you really do intend a longer report and need extra time to create it, distribute a short one quickly, commit to a time frame for the longer report, and then complete the longer report before you promised. Make certain that everyone on your internal team who either attended the event and/or works with these customers is included in the distribution list, especially in professional organizations or business-to-business products, because people who work directly with customers get very nervous when information is sent to their customers without their knowledge or approval.

INNOVATION GAMES AND CUSTOMER-CENTRIC NEW PRODUCT INNOVATION PROCESSES

Customer-centric innovation refers to the various techniques that companies employ to drive product and service innovations through interactions with customers. The process is similar to directed market research in that you're acquiring data from targeted participants that will be used to drive actionable results, and most of the discussion in the previous session applies directly, including the details of organizing the event, selecting the games, organizing the team, and processing the results.

There are several key differences, however. These include motivation, context, and overarching process. In customer-centric innovation, the primary motivation is new product development. Companies engaging in this form of inquiry are expecting new products and services as the result, or, at the very least, substantial changes and improvements to existing ones. Innovation Games are a great fit because the foundation of innovation is customer understanding.

Another key difference is the underlying context. In the previous section, one of the subtle assumptions was that you were most likely playing the games with existing customers. Thus, the context of the inquiry is grounded in an existing customer relationship. This can be contrasted with customer-centric innovation, which, despite the name, doesn't actually require an existing relationship with customers.

A third key difference is that the market research process previously described is designed to be used to accomplish a variety of goals. For example, I used the market research process with a group of vice presidents of engineering and CIOs and the *Product Box* game to identify their "ideal" developer as part of the market research I was doing for a keynote at a conference. In the introduction, Andre Gous used *Product Box* to help identify the ideal car for his daughter. In contrast, customer-centric innovation processes are focused on a single goal: new product development. To help maintain this focus, they often are based on "gated" processes, in which concepts are subjected to a series of well-defined gates and transformations as they progress from idea to product (see Figure 1.25). In gated processes, Innovation Games are most often used during the *Ideation* phase to generate promising ideas that are then screened among several

dimensions. During the ideation phase, the market research process previously described is adapted, as described next.

Ideation Phase

The use of Innovation Games in the Ideation phase tends to favor the selection of games that have higher degrees of open-ended explorations and/or games that enable you to better understand how customers are currently using existing products and services (either yours or your competitors'). To illustrate, you might play *Buy a Feature* if you had specific questions about features that might be in your next product release. However, if you wanted to explore the idea of creating a new product offering, perhaps based on some core elements of your existing product, you might instead play *Prune the Product Tree* because this game provides a greater opportunity for open-ended exploration. Games such as *The Apprentice*, *Me and*

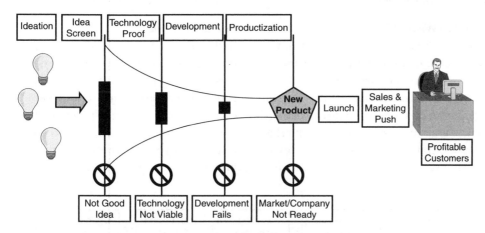

FIGURE 1.25 A Gate-Based Customer-Centric Innovation Process

My Shadow, Show and Tell, Spider Web and *Product Box* are all excellent candidates for creating ideas that feed the ideation process.

The processes associated with the Ideation phase can be further organized as shown in Figure 1.26. Clearly, these resemble the market research process described earlier, but with a few key differences.

Project Kickoff

In the market research process, a formalized kickoff meeting was presented as an optional activity. In customer-centric innovation, it is nearly required. A kickoff meeting allows the cross-functional team to review goals, establish necessary operating plans, discuss the use of Innovation Games and other techniques in the context of the larger product development process, and prepare for the possible outcomes of the research. Although kickoff meetings can still exhibit quite a range in formality and ceremony, I believe that they are essential when initiating a program of customer-centric innovation.

Where Are We Now?

This phase of the project allows the team to prepare for innovation by gaining a solid understanding of the current products and services. This is traditional "MBA-type" stuff, ranging from clear descriptions of existing products and services, brand, target markets, marketing strategies, sales processes, pricing, product or service road map, competitive landscape, and so forth. Teams should explore their companies' relationships to its customers from the perspective of the customer. Helpful approaches include using your own web site, ordering products from your own company, reading product information and sales collateral, reading what others say about your product and service, and actually using your own product (a process often referred to as "dog fooding"). In the process, the team should gain an understanding of where they think they're doing well, where they'd like to improve, and how they perceive that a customer-centric innovation process can help them the most.

Fueling Innovation

This phase most closely matches the previously described market research process. It involves selecting the game, identifying participants, and playing the game. Much less emphasis should be put on trying to answer specific questions; instead, the team should be looking for new opportunities.

Processing Results

In this phase you'll follow the same general processing steps described earlier, doing such things as processing observer note cards and preparing an internal report. However, there is no strong requirement to prepare an external report, because there is the chance that your explorations may not have produced any new results or new thinking.

FIGURE 1.26 Ideation Activities in Customer-Centric Innovation

Alternatively, your team may have identified a genuinely great idea, one that you may not want to share externally until you've had the chance to properly protect it by following the intellectual property guidelines of your employer, such as submitting an invention disclosure or filing for a patent.

Organizing and Presenting Ideas

The last step in the Ideation stage is organizing and presenting your ideas to the corporate review team during the "Idea Review" gate. During this gate all ideas are reviewed against corporately defined criteria. Those deemed worthy are moved into the next phase of the development process.

Customer-Centric Innovation Summary

Innovation Games are a natural fit in the processes most associated with new product development activities. By providing nonstandard ways to understand the "voice of the customer," they enable new product teams to focus on generating the understanding of customers that leads to truly innovative products and services.

USING INNOVATION GAMES TO FEED PRODUCT REQUIREMENTS

As described in the overview of Part One, there are many varied ways to manage product requirements. These range from developing personas, scenarios, and use cases, to using Kano analysis to identify customer needs, and to creating and managing "nonfunctional requirements," to name just a few. Innovation Games feed all these processes by allowing you to explore the world from the perspective of your customer, with your customer.

Using Innovation Games with Customer Advisory Boards

A *Customer Advisory Board* (CAB) is a specially selected group of customers, executives, and/or industry professionals who meet regularly with a company to provide in-depth feedback, guidance, and support for matters of tactical and strategic importance to a company. They are given considerable influence on the direction of products and services and are often compensated for their services.

One of the ongoing challenges of managing CABs is making certain that they don't become "rubber stamp" committees whose members sit and listen to predigested presentations without any real opportunity for substantive feedback. In other words, the amount of time you spend *listening* to your CAB should be far greater than the amount of time you spend *talking* to your CAB. Fortunately, Innovation Games are a powerful way to engage your CAB and generate fresh insights for you—and for them.

Innovation Games breathe new life into existing CABs by helping your CAB members find creative and fun ways to express themselves. Instead of sitting through a boring set of PowerPoint presentations and discussions of strategy, CAB members playing Innovation Games are actively engaged in sharing their knowledge. They also provide a powerful way to safely experiment with the games. For example, you might try a different version of a game with your CAB before playing it with other customers. And you can focus quantitative market research based on the qualitative feedback you receive from the CAB.

Table 1.5 provides specific suggestions for games to try at your next CAB meeting.

No matter what game you play, keep the rest of the Innovation Game process the

---

Ways to Refer to Customer Advisory Boards

While the specific responsibilities of a customer advisory board may vary, they are united in creating a forum for in-depth, qualitative market research. There are many ways to refer to a customer advisor board. Here are a few.

Company	Term
QUALCOMM Wireless Business Solutions	Product Strategy Council
Aladdin Knowledge Systems	Security Council
Emerson Climate Technologies	Technology Advisory Council
Wyse Technologies, Inc.	Customer Advisory Board
ILOG	Technical Advisory Board
Autodesk	Customer Council

Table 1.5 Suggested Games for a CAB Meeting

Game	Choosing Innovation Games for a CAB
Product Box	Product Box is consistently ranked as one of the most fun Innovation Games. The open-ended and sometimes silly nature of Product Box sets a great tone for a CAB and lets you gain powerful insights into what customers value from your products.
Buy a Feature	Normally, customers playing Buy a Feature purchase features according to their interests. CAB members, on the other hand, are often able to "act as if" they are a different kind of customer, allowing for a richer discussion of features.
Start Your Day	Start Your Day is usually played using calendars and other materials that you create. In a CAB, you can explain the game to your customers and ask them to bring calendars that they can share with other customers. This enriches the game on multiple dimensions, including providing you with valuable insights into how your customers manage time.
Show and Tell	One of the drawbacks of Show and Tell is that it ranks relatively high on customer preparation requirements. CAB members, because of their strong commitment to the CAB, can be counted on to do the preparation work necessary to make this game a success.
Give Them a Hot Tub	One of the concerns that product teams express over playing Give Them a Hot Tub is that they might look too "silly" or "crazy" if they share so-called outrageous features with normal customers. This fear may at times be justified with normal customers, but not with CAB members, who typically look forward to pushing product boundaries. Don't be surprised if they become disappointed when you don't push them hard enough!
Remember the Future	The core element of Remember the Future is projecting yourself forward far enough to create meaningful strategic discussions. Who better to help you do this than your CAB?

same. This should be relatively easy because you will likely have someone managing the planning function of the CAB meeting. To this you may need to add a greeter, a facilitator, a helper, observers, and an event photographer.

It is also important to share with your CAB the results of your report. You may want to consider a more open and direct approach in writing the report, including providing CAB members with access to observer notes. Finally, make certain that you provide a way for CAB members to provide feedback to you—and other CAB members—on any reports that you send. Sometimes the conversations after the CAB meeting are even more important than the conversations at

the CAB meeting because you and your CAB have had time to think more carefully about what was discussed.

SUMMARY

Customer Advisory Boards, customer-centric innovation, requirements gathering, and directed market research all benefit from the fun, exciting ways to develop a deeper understanding of your customer embodied in Innovation Games. Now that you have a solid understanding of how to integrate the use of Innovation Games into all these processes, you're ready to move on to a detailed exploration of each game so that you can pick the best game to accomplish your goals.

Part Two
THE GAMES

Now that you've completed the groundwork of Part One, you're ready for a detailed description of each of the games profiled in this book. We'll use the format outlined in Table 2.1.

Table 2.1 Structure of the Games

The Game	A Description of the Game
Why It Works	The reasons behind the game's effectiveness
Preparing for the Game	Tips to help you prepare for this game
Materials	A checklist of any game-specific materials[1]
Playing the Game	Tips to help you play this game
Processing the Results	Some suggestions for processing the results
How I Can Use This Game	A place for you to make notes on how you can use this game

1. General materials checklists recommended for all games are included in Part Three.

The detailed descriptions of the games also include several figures, photos, and sidebars, which will help you better understand how you can use the games to accomplish your goals.

Prune the Product Tree

Shape Your Product to Market Needs

Gardeners prune trees to control their growth. Sometimes the pruning is artistic, and we end up with shrubs shaped like animals or interesting abstract shapes. Much of the time the pruning is designed to build a balanced tree that yields high-quality fruit. The process isn't about "cutting," it is about "shaping." Use this metaphor to help create the product your customers desire.

THE GAME

Start by drawing a large tree on a whiteboard or butcher paper or printing a graphic image of a tree as a large format poster. Thick limbs represent major areas of functionality within your system. The inside of the tree contains leaves that represent features in the current release. Leaves that are placed at the outer edge of the canopy represent new features. The edge of the tree represents the future. Write potential new features on several index cards, ideally shaped as leaves. Ask your customers to place desired features around the tree, shaping its growth. Do they structure a tree that is growing in a balanced manner? Does one branch, perhaps a core feature of the product, get the bulk of the growth? Does an underutilized aspect of the tree become stronger? We know that the roots of a tree (your support and customer care infrastructure) need to extend at least as far as its canopy. Do yours?

WHY IT WORKS

One of the greatest challenges in creating and managing a product is creating a balanced picture of everything that must be done to be successful. The problem can be complicated by overly linear, inorganic representations of product road maps, which tend to represent product evolution as linear over time. By tapping into our understanding that products must grow in a planned way, and that products are supported by a variety of mechanisms, *Prune the Product Tree* allows customers to shape all aspects of the product, instead of just providing feedback on a selected set of features in a road map.

You and your customers both know that features vary in importance. We tend to want to put our efforts behind the most important features—those features that provide the greatest value to customers. Unfortunately, sometimes this means that we put too little effort behind the features that are needed to complete the product. The *Prune the Product Tree* game provides your customers with a way to provide explicit input into the decision-making process by looking at the set of features that compose the product in a holistic manner.

Prune the Product Tree also gives product teams the rare opportunity to identify, and potentially remove, those product features that are simply not meeting customer needs.

PREPARING FOR THE GAME

The first step in preparing for the game is selecting your tree and deciding how you want it drawn. You can have a graphic artist draw the tree, or you can draw the tree by hand. If you choose to have a graphic artist draw the tree, be careful about how nicely they draw it. One of the goals of this game is to have customers mark up the tree, and if something is

Open-Ended Exploration

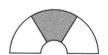

Time Frame of Action

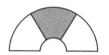

Scalability

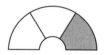

Customer Preparation

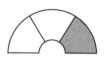

Market Preparation

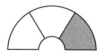

Physical Preparation

drawn too nicely customers may resist marking it up.

You'll need to prepare one tree for each group of customers. A good size for a customer group is between 5 and 10 people.

You'll also have to consider how your product is evolving over time. Stable products can be characterized by broad limbs and consistently growing canopies. I've provided a sample drawing of this kind of product (see Figure 2.2). The differently colored canopies represent various product releases. In this kind of tree you will want a way to let customers "prune" features that aren't working for them, even if they are part of the already released product. You can do this by representing these as leaves that can be removed. New features can be added to outer growth rings.

Young products can benefit from having multiple trees, especially when the branches that represent major aspects of the product may be in a state of flux. In this case, draw one tree for each version of the product, with branches appropriate to that release. Then,

Picking Your Tree Shape

One of the best parts of preparing for *Prune the Product Tree* is considering the kind of tree that best represents your product. Are you a fast growing cottonwood? A slow but steady oak? Are you a fruit-bearing tree? Do you provide shade? Comfort? Beauty? What kind of tree would your customer pick? Why? Here are some images of various trees to help get you started.

For even more inspiration consider ordering the *National Register of Big Trees* from http://www.americanforests.org/resources/bigtrees/. I'm especially fond of the Seven Sisters live oak, a 1,200 year old tree that survived Hurricane Katrina.

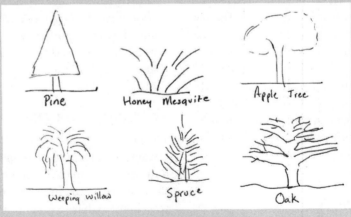

FIGURE 2.1 Sample Tree Shapes

in the "new" version of the tree, allow your customers to draw the branches that they think are most appropriate.

FIGURE 2.2 Sample Drawing of a Product Tree

Don't get hung up on drawing a perfect picture. I was working with a client who wanted to use this technique, and they seemed to be stuck on how to get started. I sketched out the tree used in the sample drawing in a few minutes on a regular piece of paper, scanned it into my computer, colored it with a simple drawing tool, and then printed it on a larger format printer as a 6'×6' poster, one tree per group.

When you're finished selecting your basic tree shape, you'll have to consider the leaves.[2] Existing features that you want customers to consider pruning (by taking them off the tree) should be printed on paper and attached to the tree with tape or re-adhesive glue. New features that you want customers to consider adding to the tree should be printed and placed around the tree. It is a good practice to list the feature on the front of the leaf and the perceived benefit on the back. You'll also want to include blank leaves to capture new ideas.

The ratio of blank leaves to predefined feature leaves reflects the degree to which you want customers to provide you with new information (things you haven't thought of or heard before) versus the degree to which you want them to arrange your existing plans. More blank leaves means that customers can add their own ideas. More predefined leaves means that customers will spend time organizing your suggestions. Either approach is okay.

Work in small teams to shape your tree.
FIGURE 2.3 Playing Prune the Product Tree

If you intend to have a large number of predefined leaves (more than a dozen, for example), consider sending the list of features along with a brief description of the same to customers in advance so that they can become familiar with them before the event. Note that having a large number of leaves usually slows down the playing of the

---

2. You can also use pine cones, fruit, or nuts, depending on the kind of tree that you choose.

game, as customers spend more time thinking about what the leaves mean and less time adding or removing leaves.

Game play is enhanced when you use index cards that are cut into the shape of a leaf or have an image of a leaf printed as a watermark. It is okay to mix leaf styles; on one project we started by using a watermark of a maple leaf but found a teacher's supply store that sold leaf-shaped cutouts. They worked great together (see the sidebar "Using Multiple Trees at the AIPMM PMEC 2006 Conference").

In terms of inviting customers, you should emphasize customers who have been using your product long enough to provide solid feedback on future developments based on how your product has evolved in the past.

The last major element of your tree is its root system: the services, support, and related corporate infrastructure (websites, partners, distribution channels, and so forth) that they would want in a vibrant, healthy tree. Such corporate infrastructure is less subject to change than product features, and you may want to consider preprinting the trees with this infrastructure.

Materials

❑ Trees, printed in poster-print format or ready to be drawn on butcher paper or a white board

❑ Preprinted leaf cards

❑ Blank leaf cards

❑ Leaf stickers (customers can put these on leaves to signify importance)

❑ Stickers and/or other artwork that help you establish the right tone

PLAYING THE GAME

Organize your participants so that 4 to 10 people are at each tree. Having too many people at a single tree prevents good group interaction. It is ideal if you can allocate one observer to each tree.

During your explanation remind participants that the shape of the tree represents growth over time. Existing features should therefore go near the trunk, as they are the oldest. The next closest leaves represent features to add in the near term. Leaves on the outer edges of the tree, at the edge of the canopy, and even beyond are considered longer term. You can make this even more explicit by putting time frames or release identifiers on the growing canopy.

Allow each group time to present their results to the entire group. Encourage other participants to ask questions about how the leaves in the tree were organized.

Try not to worry about the tree becoming unbalanced. It might happen, but my experience is that participants tend to organize features according to the shape of the tree you've given to them. In one game, a participant remarked to another, "We've got to move some features around, as the tree is becoming lopsided," and another remarked, "We're cramming too many features into this release—what can we push out?" Of course, the tree your customers create might not match the tree that they started with. If that happens, pay attention to what your customers are trying to tell you.

Encourage participants to group leaves or draw lines between leaves to clarify relationships among features. As described in the

Using Multiple Trees at the AIPMM PMEC 2006 Conference

The Association for International Product Marketing and Product Management (www.aipmm.com) used multiple trees to gather feedback from attendees at their 2006 Product Management Educational Conference. In this photo from the conference you can see three trees (see Figure 2.4). The top left tree represents the 2005 conference, which had two primary tracks (represented as two branches): Product Management and Product Marketing. The 2006 conference tree is shown below the 2005 tree and has four branches representing the phases of the product life cycle: Plan, Build, Launch, and Sustain. Tutorials, keynotes, and activities were represented as leaves that could be moved to the new tree.

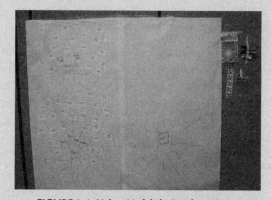

FIGURE 2.4 Using Multiple Product Trees

The 2007 tree is shown to the right. As you can see, it allowed for a completely open-ended exploration of the next conference. PMEC attendees could create their own branches, move leaves from the 2005 and 2006 trees to the 2007 tree, and add new leaves (representing new topics they'd like to see addressed at the 2007 conference). There is also a package of leaf shaped foil stickers, which attendees used to indicate strong support for a proposed topic. Attendees were also encouraged to personalize their trees, adding business cards or other mementos of their time at the conference.

PMEC participants quickly got into the game, as you can see in Figure 2.5. Groups quickly formed, mostly from people who shared the same lunch tables. These groups moved the leaves representing the talks that they liked most from the 2005 and 2006 conferences to the 2007 conference, and, as you can see, they added several new ideas for talks by adding new leaves. Participants added business cards and one even drew a heart around two leaves that she particularly "loved."[3]

FIGURE 2.5 Playing Prune the Product Tree at PMEC

Therese Padilla, Executive Director of AIPMM, posted her experience of the event into the Enthiosys Forum at www.innovationgames.com. Here is an excerpt from her post:

"Once the trees were placed around the room and the conference attendees began to add ideas, it was gratifying to scan the room and visually see all the new ideas that were placed on the trees. We have begun to gather the results, but already we have three exceptional ideas for our next conference.

This is a wildly different approach to conference activities. This form of engagement energized the attendees and really involved them. This was the first time in all our conferences that we witnessed this level of participation and creativity from attendees. Attendees really took an interest in the event and were encouraged to make the event their own. This was the best way to ask them to design PMEC the way they wanted to see the content."

3. This is an example of when it was good that an observer spoke; by asking the meaning of the "heart," the observer was able to confirm that the participant "loved" the talks.

sidebar about the PMEC conference, one participant drew a heart around a pair of leaves to signify that she "loved" these features.

Encourage participants to personalize their trees. Although not required, the game can be more fun when people add additional art (birds, grass, sun), tape business cards to the trunk, or write their name on the back of their leaf suggestions.

Don't forget about the root system. Encourage participants to write information into the root system.

Try to leave the trees up as long as possible. If you're playing this game over a multiday event, put the trees up on the first day and leave them up as long as possible. You'll find that participants continue to play the game as they think of more leaves and discuss the game with other participants.

PROCESSING THE RESULTS

Depending on the number of participants, you'll have between one and seven trees, each adorned with leaves, along with the notes of the observers. Compare the results of this exercise to your current product road map and look for the following items.

- Which of your features were pruned? Although you might have a strong attachment to some (or even all) of these features, you should carefully consider removing them to allow for other features that have more customer demand.

- Do the trees retain their general shape? Customers who put a lot of leaves on a single branch can be telling you that you

haven't been paying attention to a critical feature set. Customers who change the shape of the tree can be providing even richer feedback about how they perceive your company.

- How fast do customers want your tree to grow? Customers who put a lot of features on the inner versions (or releases) may be signaling that you're not releasing your product fast enough or often enough. Alternatively, fewer leaves in the interior may mean that the current plans are just fine, but look for the growth in the canopy, which might hold some really big new features.

- What things do customers add to or remove from your root system? How do these relate to your current infrastructure? Pay special attention to this information because it usually is of critical significance to your customers.

How I Can Use Prune the Product Tree

_____

_____

_____

_____

_____

_____

_____

_____

_____

_____

_____

_____

_____

_____

_____

_____

_____

_____

Remember the Future

Understand Your Customers' Definition of Success

"What should our product do?" Ah, yes, the seemingly open-ended question that many times isn't that open ended at all. Most of the time, what your product should do is some reasonable extrapolation of what it has done in the past. Your cell phone should have better signal strength, longer battery life, and be lighter. So should your laptop. And your car should be safer, faster, more stylish, and get better gas mileage. The question "What should our product do?" is therefore often trivially answered: "Your product should be better." Which should make you wonder, are you asking the right question? And are you asking it in the right way?

The Game

Hand each of your customers a few pieces of paper. Ask them to imagine that it is sometime in the future and that they've been using your product almost continuously between now and that future date (it could be a month, quarter, year, or, for strategic planning purposes, five years or even a decade—pick a time frame that is appropriate for your research goals). Now, ask them to go even further—an extra day, week, month. Ask your customer to write down, in as much detail as possible, exactly what your product will have done to make them happy (or successful or rich or safe or secure or smart; choose the set of adjectives that works best for your product).

Note: The phrasing of the question is extremely important. You'll get different results if you ask "What should the system do?" instead of "What will the system have done?" (If you're skeptical, just try it.)

Why It Works

This game is based on numerous studies in cognitive psychology that have examined how we think about the future. When we ask the question "What will our product do?" we're left with an open-ended future, one in which every possible future is equally plausible. Of course, this isn't strictly true, and to answer the question we will pick a possible future and describe it. However, the lack of a concrete outcome means that we don't have to deal with the details of how our product will have done it. Others will tend to judge our answers as "hollow" or "lacking substance," because there is no requirement that this is actually the future that will materialize.

The results change rather dramatically when we alter the wording of the question. When we ask "What will our product have done?" we are thinking of a future event as one that already has occurred—"remembering" the future. Because this event is "in the past," we must mentally generate a sequence of events that caused this event to have occurred. We not only have a more concrete idea of what the product did, we can begin to answer the question "How did the product do it?" Others will tend to judge our answers as more richly detailed, more sensible, and more plausible, precisely because if an outcome or future is thought of as already accomplished, it can be more easily described.

This isn't to say that the event we envision will actually occur, or that each customer who plays the game will generate the same result. Actually predicting the future is not really the purpose of *Remember the Future*

Open-Ended Exploration

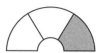

Time Frame of Action

Scalability

Customer Preparation

Market Preparation

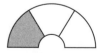

Physical Preparation

Remember the Future—From 1997!

I often use *Remember the Future* whenever I want to generate a detailed plan of how I'm going to successfully complete a project, from planning the release of a software project, closing a large or complex sale, preparing for a conference, or even planning an Innovation Game (as suggested in Part One). The earliest picture I have of using *Remember the Future* to help plan events is a Polaroid from Dave Smith, who facilitated this game for the Aurigin team in 1997 to plan the installation of a complex software system (Figure 2.6 is a scan of that Polaroid). The project was successfully completed, in large part because this game enabled everyone to focus on the specific sequence of events that resulted in a fully deployed system.

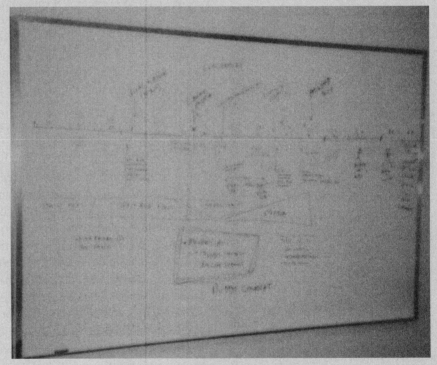

FIGURE 2.6 Remember the Future from 1997

(although if you have success in doing this, please let me know). What is important is that *Remember the Future* enables you to not only understand your customers' definition of success, but also their understanding of how that successful outcome happened.

PREPARING FOR THE GAME

It helps to draw a timeline to make certain you're really remembering a future event as if it were the past. In Figure 2.7, the current date is February 2. In step 1, we project forward into the future to March 30 and ask our customer to remember their use of our product as of March 15 (a date that is in the future).

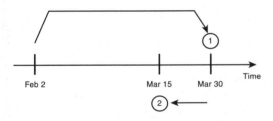

FIGURE 2.7 A Timeline Helps You Plan for Remember the Future

Vary the timeline to get different results. If you want to understand more about your near-term product plans, choose weeks, months, or quarters. If you want to understand more about how customers envision very general topics or issues regarding strategic evolution, consider projecting a decade or more into the future.

Practice how you phrase the question and how you present the game to your customers.

This is especially important, as outlined in the sidebar "Framing the Question."

You can structure this game to deal with more than one question. This approach is suitable for strategic planning purposes, when you have multiple facets of the future that you want to explore. This also allows this game to scale to rather large group sizes.

Consider letting customers know about the broad topics you'd like to explore before the game to allow them to mentally prepare for the game.

Materials

❑ One easel with flip chart paper for each group of customers playing the game, plus an additional easel for the facilitator

PLAYING THE GAME

Because this game is one of the easiest to play, there isn't a lot of need for detailed advice. But don't be misled by the simplicity of the game—the magic lies in the discussion of how your customers perceive their future. To get to this discussion, you can

- Encourage customers to work individually, letting them know that at the end of the game each will be asked to present their results to the group.

- Request that customers work as a group, which is useful for when you want a chosen group of customers to work together answering a common question. If you choose this option, appoint a group leader who is responsible for capturing the results of the group and being the spokesperson during the discussion phase.

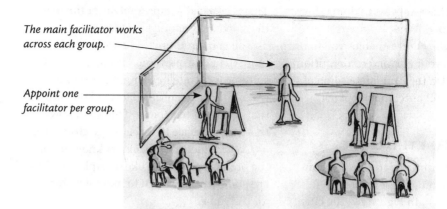

The main facilitator works across each group.

Appoint one facilitator per group.

FIGURE 2.8 Playing Remember the Future with Multiple Groups

It is the Richness of Detail That Matters

What distinguishes *Remember the Future* from simply asking about a future event is the level of detail that customers generate when answering questions framed in the future tense of the verb. Suppose, for example, that we'd like to get a sense about who will win the next FIFA World Cup.

The simplest way to frame the question is, "Who will win the next FIFA World Cup?" Asked this way, you're likely to answer with just enough detail to justify your prediction: "France emerged as the lone European country to make it through the quarter-finals through a combination of excellent goal tending and solid free kicks. They easily won their semi-finals and turned in a great match in the finals."

Framing it in the future-perfect tense results in, "Imagine that it is the day after the next FIFA World Cup. Who will have won?" You might also say France, but notice that right away your mind is drawn to answering *why did France win?* The easiest way to put your mind at ease it to answer

that question. And the more detail you put into answering the question, the better you feel.

The end result is often more like, "France was the unlikely winner after a grueling set of matches played over several weeks. Their goalkeeper was spectacular in the first round, establishing the French team as the team to beat. In the quarter-finals, the French goal keeper made more than 12 saves, giving his team confidence to aggressively and relentlessly attack Brazil, resulting in the lone and deciding goal in the 80th minute of play. The aggressive play continued in the semi-finals, where the French outscored Argentina 3 to nil. Finally, the combination of aggressive attacking and continued brilliant goal tending allowed the French to beat Mexico 2 to 1 in the finals."

It is important to note that in both cases we can see plausible explanations of how the future will unfold. The second example, however, contains the rich and detailed explanations of the future that you can leverage to better understand your customers' definition of success.

- Encourage customers to work any way they choose, either individually or as a team.

During the presentation phase, give a few minutes for each person to describe his or her answers. Then explicitly invite other participants to comment on this particular version of the future.

Processing the Results

The primary processing step for this game is to compare your current product development road maps with your newfound understanding of how your customers perceive their future. The following areas are worthy of exploration:

- To what extent do your road maps result in a product that meets your customers' perceptions of their future requirements?
- To what extent do your customers' vision of their future significantly alter your plans? How? Why?

How I Can Use Remember the Future

_____

_____

_____

_____

_____

_____

_____

_____

_____

_____

Spider Web

Understand Product Relationships

All products and services coexist within a larger context of an ecosystem of related, complementary, and even competitive products and services. Unfortunately, product designers often fail to recognize and leverage the relationships within this ecosystem. This often means they miss innovative opportunities to create happier customers *and* capture more revenue. The *Spider Web* game helps you understand how your customer sees the relationships between your product and service and other products and services. You can then use this information to capture more revenue by creating innovations around these relationships.

One kind of innovation occurs when you realize that you can do more with your current product. This discovery often leads you to change your product's boundary, or the demarcation between your product and other products, or between recommended and actual usage. Of course, the creator of the product or service is not usually the person who discovers the new usage. I don't think that Proctor and Gamble intended for Bounce Fabric Softener Sheets to be used for dissolving soap scum from shower doors or for wiping up sawdust from a woodworking shop, but these are common alternative uses for Bounce.[4]

Another kind of innovation occurs when you realize that you can create a better total solution by establishing partnerships between your offering and other offerings. A

4. See http://mountainsurvival.com/bounce.html or http://www.asktheladies.com/the-magic-of-fabric-softener-sheets.htm.

financial-services firm might partner with an estate-planning firm to create a better total solution for families with young children. A yogurt maker might partner with a cereal manufacturer to create a healthy new snack that leverages both brands. A human resources software vendor might integrate its application with a payroll provider to eliminate errors that occur through redundant data entry.

THE GAME

Put the name of your product or service in the center of a circle. Ask your customers to draw other products and services that they think are related to your product. As they draw these products and services, ask them to tell you when, how, and why these are used. Ask them to draw lines between the different products and services. Encourage them to use different colors, weights, or styles to capture important relationships (for example, important relationships can be drawn with a thicker line or a different color pen). The *Spider Web* game works well with the *Start Your Day* game. After your customers review when and where they use your offering, you can explore in a subsequent session the various relationships that exist between the different products and services that they use throughout the day.

WHY IT WORKS

Although you may think you have a solid understanding of how your product or service relates to other products and services, chances are your customers have a different

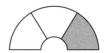

Open-Ended Exploration

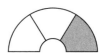

Time Frame of Action

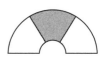

Scalability

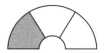

Customer Preparation

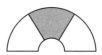

Market Preparation

Physical Preparation

point of view. By helping you understand these relationships from their perspective, *Spider Web* helps you capture more revenue by showing you webs of potentially unknown relationships.

Spider Web is partially inspired by a requirements-analysis technique called *context diagramming*. Context diagramming was originally created to show the data that flows between a given software system and other entities with which this system communicates. These entities can be people, other software systems, physical devices, electromechanical devices, other sensors, and so forth. Context diagrams are a useful tool, usually created by business analysts trained to interpret the perceptions of a customer and who usually manage to make their context diagrams look very neat and tidy.

Skilled professionals who create context diagrams often face special challenges when working directly with customers. One challenge is that customers tend to create pretty messy diagrams, especially when working in groups, and the messiness can make business analysts uneasy. Another challenge is that because business analysts have often studied the problem domain before working directly with customers, they bring their own expectations of how the diagrams should look to the game. The worst situation is when business analysts attempt to guide customers into creating diagrams that match their expectations ("Don't you think your car should be drawn with a connection to your portable music player?"). The best approach in this situation is to include your business analysts as observers and empower your facilitator to keep them quiet during the game.

Spider Web, on the other hand, encourages customers to directly draw *their* view of the relationships. And because the real world isn't a neat and tidy place, customer-generated diagrams tend to get messy. Wonderfully messy. Realistically messy. Messy in a way that helps you understand the real opportunities for genuine innovation.

PREPARING FOR THE GAME

The key step in preparing for *Spider Web* is preparing the kinds of relationships you'd like customers to explore. Suggestions include the following:

- Corporate relationships—How your customers perceive relationships between your company and other companies they use, which is useful in identifying potential partners and enhanced service opportunities. Example: Customers may perceive or desire a relationship between the manufacturer of laundry detergent and the manufacturer of a washing machine.

- Location/environmental relationships— The relationship of your product to the environment or location in which it is used, in all facets of use. Example: Laundry detergent has location relationship with a washing machine (typically nearby) and area of the home where laundry is done.

- Operating relationships—The relationship of your product to other products it uses, leverages, or requires to accomplish the total task of your customer. Example: Laundry detergent has an operating relationship with a washing machine.

- Human relationships—The relationship of your product to the people who may or do use it. Example: Laundry detergent is used typically used by the person putting dirty clothes into the washing machine.

- Role relationships—The relationship of your product to the people who interact with it based on various roles. These relationships are often correlated with various process steps and/or responsibilities within a corporation. Example: Laundry detergent may not be used by the person folding the laundry.

This is not an exhaustive list, and you should carefully consider the specific kind of relationships you want to explore while preparing to play *Spider Web*. It is best to present two to four possible relationships to customers and let them choose which they want to explore in greater detail.

Create one or two spider webs in your internal product team before doing this exercise with customers. You'll find that the results are probably useful in their own right, and it will prepare you for what you might see from your customers.

Materials

There are no special materials for this game.

The Universal Remote Control Warm-Up Exercise

The "ideal remote control" warm-up exercise can help customers better understand the goals of this game.

"What does your ideal universal remote control look like? What do you want it to be connected to or control in your house or apartment?"

Get customers started by drawing a simple remote control connected to a few devices and invite them to complete the picture.

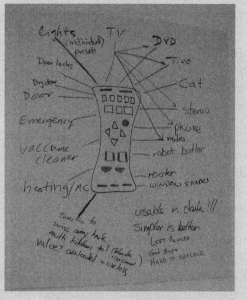

FIGURE 2.9 Universal Remote

PLAYING THE GAME

Give customers the option of working alone or in teams. Although the game typically produces the most interesting results when customers work as a group, the nature of exploring relationships can be personal, and some customers will be more comfortable working alone.

Encourage your customers to draw lines with different colors, weights, and styles. Annotate the lines with as much information as possible; more information fuels innovation and helps you in post-processing the results.

Encourage your customers to include any affected company, system, role, or person. When you review these diagrams with your customer, ask them for names, titles, motivations, and so forth.

You may find that your spider web resembles a process-flow or supply-chain diagram. That's okay.

Try putting the *Spider Web* game together with the *Start Your Day* game by asking customers if they can think of or can draw different webs at different times of the day, the week, the month, or the quarter.

Try varying the location of where the product is used when asking customers to draw their web. Do you think business executives would draw the same spider web for a laptop computer when they're using it on a plane as compared to when they're using it in their office or at their home?

When your customers are finished creating their spider webs, ask them to describe the webs to the group. Encourage customers to directly ask questions and see which customers resonate with various relationships.

PROCESSING THE RESULTS

The relationships captured in *Spider Web* diagrams don't often provide definitive answers. Instead, they provide starting points for further, more detailed discussions. Here are some questions that you can use to help you process the results:

- What kind of entities are related to your product? Are they people? Objects? Locations? Conceptual ideas? Other companies? How can you leverage these relationships to create more revenue?

- What kind of relationship was created by your customer? Are you sharing work products or artifacts, as in a supply chain? Are the products sharing data?

- Do the entities represent areas you should explore to gain a better understanding of your customer? Keep in mind that anything you find surprising should be strongly considered for further exploration.

- Do the relationships represent current reality? Are they part of a planned future? Or do they represent a potential future?

- What happens if you change the focus of control between your product and other products drawn by your customer?

How I Can Use Spider Web

_____

_____

_____

_____

_____

_____

_____

_____

_____

_____

_____

_____

_____

_____

_____

_____

_____

Product Box

Identify the Most Exciting Product Features

The aisles of supermarkets around the world are filled with colorful product boxes from all over the world. They tell us of products that are new. Improved. New *and* improved. They tell us how these products will make us thinner, smarter, sleeker, happier. In the process, the best boxes help move that box from the shelf and into our home.

Product Box lets you leverage your customers' collective retail consumer experiences by asking them to design a box for your product. Not just any box, but a box that represents the product that *they* want to buy. In the process, you'll learn what your customers think are the most important, exciting features of a given product or service.

The Game

Ask your customers to imagine that they're selling your product at a trade show, retail outlet, or public market. Give them a few cardboard boxes and ask them to design the product box that they would buy. The box can contain anything they want—marketing slogans that they find interesting, pictures, price points. They can build elaborate boxes through the materials you'll provide or just write down the phrases and slogans they find most interesting. When finished, ask your customer to use *their* box to sell *your product* to *you* and the other customers in the room.

Why It Works

Regardless of what you tell them, customers want to believe that the product or service that they're buying is going to solve their problems. Not just the problems that you told them they have during the sales process, but the real problems that are driving their purchase. In some cases, these may match. In others, customers, even during the sale, may not be able to fully understand, much less articulate, the problems that are driving their behavior. *Product Box* gives customers a way to tap into these deep needs and express them when they are selling *their* product back to you.

Although your customers are trying to sell you, they will also be selling to the other customers in the room. Watching the interaction among customers is often where you can identify the most important and useful information. Who nods in agreement? Who shakes their head? When? Who asks questions? About what? What messages resonate with other customers?

The reactions of other customers in the room help overcome one of the more common challenges faced by product teams: focusing on benefits instead of features. The advantage of *selling* the box is that, even if your customers have written a feature on their box, chances are good that they will *sell* it by promoting the benefits.

Preparing for the Game

This game has a lot of physical preparation, so make certain you allocate enough time. You need to protect all the tables customers will be using; cover them with either butcher paper, plastic table cloth, or easel paper, because customers are going to be creating boxes using glue, markers, and other messy

Open-Ended Exploration

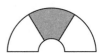

Time Frame of Action

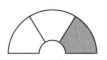

Scalability

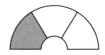

Customer Preparation

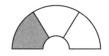

Market Preparation

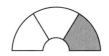

Physical Preparation

materials. Providing paper is recommended because it allows customers to sketch ideas before working on their product box. Save this paper—you can often obtain additional insights by looking at the "doodles" and sketches that customers create on the table as they create their boxes. Paper also contributes to an enjoyable experience because it clearly signals that they're going to have fun.

Use relatively large plain white boxes; 12"×5"×13" or similar size works well. But the size shouldn't be much larger, because part of the magic is in constraining the amount of room that people have to create their boxes.

Bring enough blank boxes to allow everyone to create his or her own box and include a few extra to support experimentation. You won't need all of them; some customers will spontaneously form small groups and work together to create their box. That is okay. Paradoxically, it doesn't work the other

---

Product Box, Vision Box, and Extreme Data Sheets

Techniques that might appear at the surface to be similar to *Product Box* include Jim Highsmith's *Vision Box* and Dean Leffingwell's *Extreme Data Sheet*. In Jim's *Vision Box*, development teams work together to design the box that contains their future product. Jim emphasizes the same kinds of design elements of a *Product Box*—the product name, key selling points, compelling features, and so forth. Dean recommends a similar approach, except that he uses a technical and marketing data sheet format instead of a box. Both approaches work well at the beginning of the project, when the internal development team needs to generate clarity on their goals. Like *Product Box*, they are fun and engaging, especially when internal teams are selling their box to each other.

Upon closer examination, however, there is a considerable difference between the *Product Box* Innovation Game and the *Vision Box* or *Extreme Data Sheet* exercise. In *Product Box*, the focus is external, on your customer. What do they want? How do they design the box? What images do

they use?. In *Vision Box/Extreme Data Sheet*, the focus is internal, on the internal product team. What does the internal team want? How does the internal team design the box? What images does the internal team choose?

This difference in focus also results in a different process. In *Product Box*, we celebrate the many and varied boxes that customers generate during the game, because these create a rich source of information that we can mine for innovations. In *Vision Box* or *Extreme Data Sheet*, the goal is to create a unified consensus around what the team is going to do. Thus, although many boxes or data sheets are created, the team works together until one is selected.

When you're looking to create the foundation of customer understanding that drives innovation, use the externally focused *Product Box*. When you're looking for a fun way to help an internally focused project team gain clarity about what they want to build, especially at the beginning of a project, use *Vision Box/Extreme Data Sheet*.

---

way: if you try to force customers to work together, they'll resent it and ask for their own box!

Bring at least four to six sample product boxes to illustrate what you're looking for. Cereal boxes, old consumer-class, shrink-wrapped software boxes, and cartons of yogurt are all excellent choices. Cereal boxes are especially useful because they contain several design elements that you should review with your customers to help them get started, including

- The name of the manufacturer
- The name of the product
- A "data sheet" detailing nutritional information
- Colorful characters or symbols that are designed to appeal to specific market segments (such as cartoon characters for cereals focused at children)
- Target slogans ("Heart Healthy" or "Tastes Great")
- Coupons or points to encourage repeat purchases
- Offers for "free stuff" inside the box
- Ideas on how you can spend more money ("Send $9.95 for a free watch!")

Packaging design can be as creative as product box design. If appropriate, bring product boxes that contained different products and let your customers observe how designers packaged the materials.

You might be worried that in a mixed group of customers some might be unwilling to participate because of a fear that they could give away secrets to their potential competition. As described in Part One, your best bet is to carefully screen for this up front when selecting participants, and avoid inviting customers who are direct competitors where your product is the axis of competition.

A related problem occurs when you have many shy customers who may not be interested in participating. When this is a concern, consider creating some kind of game or prize for the "best" box. Because it is almost a certainty that at least *one* person will want to win the prize, general competitive human nature will kick in, and you should find yourself with several excellent entries into your competition. If you choose to conduct a contest, let the people who are participating in the exercises be the judges. Give each person one vote; the box with the most votes wins! If you're stuck on what makes a good prize, try movie tickets.

It is especially important to include a cross-functional team in this game. Marketing, sales, and support can all benefit from seeing how customers sell your product. We've seen clients create entire customer service programs based on a slogan written on one of their customer's product boxes; this might not have happened if the customer service representative was absent from the team.

Materials

- ❑ One blank bright white product box for each participant.
- ❑ Colored markers, crayons, pencils, pens for each table.
- ❑ Glitter glue for each table.

Have Fun at Arts and Crafts and Teacher Supply Stores

One of the fun aspects of preparing for a *Product Box* game is purchasing the supplies. You can just wander around an arts and crafts, party planning, or teachers' supply store and buy stuff. I've seen customers use plastic springs, smiley faces, pipe cleaners, and glitter glue. They've cut boxes apart, taped them together, and connected them with modeling clay. Buy just about anything you want. Give it to your customers and encourage them to have some fun using it—and they will.

- Plain white and colored paper for each table.
- Stickers (stars or words or images, like "New" or "Exciting"). Check out www.innovationgames.com for ideas.
- Two or three sample boxes for each table.
- Butcher paper or easel paper for covering each table.

Playing the Game

You can think of this game being played in two phases: creating the boxes and then selling them. Start the first phase by using the sample boxes that you brought with you to explain the game. On the sample cereal boxes, point out each of the design elements listed previously.

Next, encourage people to create their own boxes. In this phase you'll get a lot questions of the form "Is it OK if I _____?" For

Innovation Games and International Product Teams

Innovation Games have been played in the United States, Mexico, Taiwan, Germany, and Great Britain with great success. The likely reason for this is that the design of the games is based on near universal principles of human psychology and organizational behavior. For example, all cultures have some degree of bartering for goods and services, making *Buy a Feature* universally accessible to participants. The boat and controlled discussion of *Speed Boat* make it similarly universally accessible. Although I don't speak Spanish, the genuine fun that participants experience when designing and selling their product boxes is clearly evident in these photos from the 2005 Samana Nacional PyME held in Mexico City, Mexico.

FIGURE 2.10 Playing Product Box at the 2005 Samana Nacional PyME

example, "Is it OK if want to cut my box?" Yes. "Is it OK if we work in teams?" Yes. "Do we have to work in teams?" No. "Can I glue two boxes together?" Yes. "Can I add stickers and tape?" Yes.

Allow about 30 to 45 minutes to create boxes. When the boxes are completed, you start the next phase of the game, in which customers sell you their boxes. Try to make certain that your customers are standing up and that you're sitting down when they are presenting their product box. This helps reinforce the different roles you're assuming.

You'll need to allow between 5 and 10 minutes for each box selling. Since you don't know which customers will form box teams, it is safest to allocate 5 minutes for each person and then adjust based on the number of boxes created. You'll also have to keep the focus on the selling process. Some facilitators use an egg timer or even a gong, and turn this into a mini-game—Who can do the best job selling their box in less than 6 minutes?

Have some observers watch the persons selling their box. Have others focus on the audience's reactions. Try to focus on the benefits expressed by the seller.

As the game progresses you'll often find that many boxes have similar slogans. Although it is tempting to have only a handful of customers sell their boxes, the reality is that everyone who has created a box will want to sell it. Manage your time accordingly.

What Happened to the Boxes?

It is especially important to photograph the boxes before customers leave, because many customers will want to take their boxes home as a souvenir.

FIGURE 2.11 Playing Product Box

Processing the Results

The open-ended nature of the game allows customers to generate a variety of potentially useful information. The first step is to transcribe and categorize the type of the textual and graphical contents on the box along with any selling statements made by customers while they were selling their box to your product team. Here are some categories to get you started:

- Feature—Statements related to a specific feature.

- Benefit—Statements related to a benefit.

- Labels or slogans—Marketing messages, statements, or titles. It is often quite interesting to see how customers repeat, change, or paraphrase your own marketing messages. You may want to separately categorize fun, fictitious "endorsement quotes" that customers often add to their boxes.

The second step is to categorize how each statement, pitch, or graphic is related to the product. Here are some secondary categories that you may find useful:

- Accolades—Something outstanding about the product or company in general. Review these to see how they should influence your marketing mix.

- Adoption—Comments on how widespread the product is used or desired. Review these to understand whether you're hitting the right segments.

- Community—Comments on elements of the user community such as websites, newsgroups, user conferences, and so

forth. Review these to understand if you've created an infrastructure that allows your customers to love your product.

- User experience—Comments related to the user experience. How easy is it for your customers to do things such as unpack, set up, configure, use, store, or otherwise interact with your product? Review these items for specific ways in which your product is perceived as superior to competing solutions.

- Support—Comments related to your support infrastructure. Positive comments here often represent a fresh way of marketing your solution.

- Technology—Comments on your product's technological foundation. Having a technology foundation that is considered so "cool" or special that customers perceive it as a selling feature is a special advantage in today's market.

- Price—Comments on the specific price, including discounts, rebates, special offers, promotions, various versions or differentiated models (for example, "Basic" vs. "Deluxe" or "Standard" vs. "Professional").

- Value—Comments on perceived value. Review these to ensure that your perception of the value provided by your products is congruent with that of your customer, and be willing to adjust your point of view as needed!

The third step is to assess the degree to which your current product matches the idealized product your company has described.

For example, suppose that customers have written positive comments about their idealized user experience. This may be because your current product has a great user experience. It could be that they are responding deeply to something they can't stand about your current offering. Thus, you must analyze the boxes with a critical eye, looking for the gems of truth that represent things your customers want in their idealized product that you're currently not providing.

When you're finished analyzing the boxes, display them in a prominent location. Looking at something created by a customer, in the customer's own handwriting, is much more compelling than reading a boring report on the session.

How I Can Use Product Box

Buy a Feature

Prioritize Features

Which feature will entice customers to purchase your product? Which feature will cause customers to upgrade? Which feature will make customers so happy that they'll ignore or tolerate the features that they wish you would fix or remove?

Product planners endlessly debate these and other kinds of questions. Choosing the right set of features to add to a release often marks the difference between short-term failure or long-term success. Unfortunately, too many product planners make this choice without involving the people most affected by it—their customers. The *Buy a Feature* game improves the quality of this decision by asking your customers to help you make it.

THE GAME

Create a list of potential features and provide each with a price. Just like for a real product, the price can be based on development costs, customer value, or something else. Although the price can be the actual cost you intend to charge for the feature, this is usually not required. Customers buy features that they want in the next release of your product using play money you give them. Make certain that some features are priced high enough that no one customer can buy them. Encourage customers to pool their money to buy especially important and/or expensive features. This will help motivate negotiations between customers as to which features are most important.

This game works best with four to seven customers in a group, so that you can create more opportunities for customers to pool

their money through negotiating. Unlike the *Product Box* game, the *Buy a Feature* game is based on the list of features that are likely to be in your development road map.

WHY IT WORKS

Product planners often fall into the trap of thinking that customers have clearly defined product priorities. Some do. Most don't. When presented with a set of options, many customers will simply say "I want them all" and put the responsibility for prioritizing their requests on your shoulders. Alternatively, product managers often gather feature priorities by working with customers one-on-one and, in the process, and perhaps without even realizing it, again take responsibility for prioritizing features. By engaging customers as a group and giving them a limited amount of resources, you give them the opportunity to prioritize their desires as a group. But that's not where the magic lies. The magic lies in structuring the conversations so that your customers are negotiating with *each other* for specific features. It is this negotiation that enhances your understanding of what your customers really want.

PREPARING FOR THE GAME

In general, group customers by similar operating characteristics instead of traditional approaches to market segmentation. To illustrate the difference, let's assume you're selling a remarkable electronic toy vehicle that is powered by a fuel cell instead of a battery, giving it substantially more power

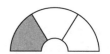

Open-Ended Exploration

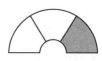

Time Frame of Action

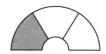

Scalability

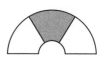

Customer Preparation

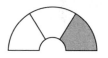

Market Preparation

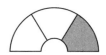

Physical Preparation

for longer periods of time. Traditional market segmentation techniques will produce groups of customers who will reference each other when buying the product, but who may use it in different ways. Because you're interested in getting feedback on how people use your product, group people who use it similarly into the same group (people who use it in a park should be in one group, whereas people who use the product at the beach should be in a different group).

One of the more time-consuming tasks in preparing for this game is preparing and pricing the features that will be available for sale. Too few features won't provide for interesting discussions. Too many can confuse customers and take too long to play. A good list is between 14 and 30 features. Each feature should include a meaningful label, a short description, and an enumeration of benefits. Avoid including features that have been committed to a release—if you know you're going to do it, why include it? Keep in mind the shorter time-to-action expectations of customers when playing this game, favoring features that can be delivered in the next one to three product versions.

The next step is pricing your features. Pricing is always one of the most challenging tasks of any product manager, and even though *Buy a Feature* is a game, pricing features for the game can be just as challenging as pricing a real product! Fortunately, you should be able to leverage all the techniques normally associated with real product and feature pricing—projected costs, customer value propositions, and so forth.

Although using projected development costs as a starting baseline is helpful, you

should price features in a way that is independent from cost if this gives you better insight into customer motivations. For example, you might have customer requests for features that you think may not be within your best strategic interest. Even if these features are easy or low cost, consider pricing them relatively high to help gauge customer desire. Alternatively, you may have expensive features that you think are quite important to your strategic future; therefore, price them lower. Finally, value-based pricing is always appropriate, and it works in *Buy a Feature*, too. Price features according to the relative and/or absolute value they provide to customers. Just keep in mind that to actually use value-based pricing you will have to complete additional market research to truly understand the value proposition of your solution, which is often a time-consuming project. It will help to remember that while you want good pricing, it is a *game*, and you don't need perfect pricing.

Feature interactions also influence pricing. Consider a feature that you project at 100dd ("development dollars") that could negatively impact your ability to secure a desired business partnership. In this case, you might price it at 300dd to justify the potential negative impact of the lost business relationship and see what happens.

Keep in mind that the foundation of this exercise is pricing features to maximize customer interaction and negotiation. Therefore, at least some features should be priced so high that no single customer can purchase the item. This will force negotiation among customers because they will have to pool their money to buy the feature.

After pricing features, you need to consider how much money you will distribute to customers. Here, again, the goal is to distribute a sum of money that helps maximize customer interaction during the game. The total amount of money for all people involved in the exercise should allow them to purchase between one-third and two-thirds of the available features. Less than one-third means that there is too little money and interaction will suffer because it is too hard to purchase features (you're overconstraining the participants). More than two-thirds means there is too much money, and interaction will suffer because it is too easy to buy features (you're underconstraining the participants). As mentioned earlier, if one customer can buy too many features, you're pricing your individual features too low.

To make planning this exercise easier, add up the total set of features and then build a simple spreadsheet so that you know how much money to give to each participant. Suppose, for example, that you create a set of 23 potential features for sale and that the total price for all of these features is 343dd. This produces a target range of 114dd to 228dd to give to each *group* of four to nine customers playing the game.

Table 2.2 can help you determine how to allocate money. The columns are the number of customers participating in the exercise. The rows represent the amount of money that you can give to each person. The cells highlighted in dark gray provide too little money to each customer, and the cells highlighted in light gray provide too much. The cells in plain white are just right.

Table 2.2 Allocating Money to Customers

Money per person	Number of people playing the game					
	4	5	6	7	8	9
15	60	75	90	105	120	135
20	80	100	120	140	160	180
25	100	125	150	175	200	225
30	120	150	180	210	240	270
35	140	175	210	245	280	315
40	160	200	240	280	320	360
45	180	225	270	315	360	405
50	200	250	300	350	400	450
55	220	275	330	385	440	495

After you've calculated how much money to give each person playing the game, you have to consider how many people may be representing a single customer, especially in business environments. For example, if you're selling or creating business-to-business products or services, it is quite common for your larger customers to send two, three, or even more people to events such as an Innovation Game. There are many ways you can handle this:

- You could require that a given customer send only one person. This is not recommended. If one of your larger customers wants to send more than one person, let them.

- You could allocate the money to the customers, letting them negotiate among themselves for their purchases. Be careful of this approach because it can negatively impact the interactions with other participants.

- You could place multiple people from a single customer into multiple groups. This is often the best solution because it allows each person to negotiate in a way that is focused on the person's own point of view and allows you to segment participants by role. For example, a software company was interested in understanding differences in feature preferences between business-oriented decision makers and technical users. In this case, each company sent two representatives—one representing business-oriented decision makers, the other technical users. Each was given the same amount of money but played the game with a group of their peers rather than with their co-worker.

- You could even vary the amount of money given to individual participants. Although I recommend that each participant be given the same amount of money, this is not an absolute rule, and you should trust your instincts relative to your customers. If you think that varying the amount of money given to participants will create a better experience, do it.

Don't forget to provide change for the facilitator. In the preceding example, suppose you elect to give 35dd to each of five people for a total of 175dd. Your facilitator should have at least 40dd in change to help the game run smoothly.

Some features may increase the retail or end price of your product. When this happens, include your realistic assessment of the increased price in your feature description.

Have some fun with preparing the money for the game. Create your own! Creating your own money is actually an advantage because you can create money with exactly the right denominations needed to play the game. Figure 2.12 shows two examples: the top from Aladdin Knowledge Systems, Inc., and the bottom from AirTransportIT. Don't become too attached to your money—customers often take it as a souvenir of the game.

Aladdin Knowledge Systems

AirTransportIT
FIGURE 2.12 Sample Play Money

You can include antagonistic or nonsensical combinations of features to see how different segments will respond. For example, suppose you are using *Buy a Feature* with something as simple as a tape dispenser. You might have one feature that makes the dispenser bigger to hold larger rolls of tape and another that makes it smaller to make it lighter and easier to use. Do either of these get purchased? If neither is purchased, the segments represented by your customers playing the game may not be interested in either feature. If they are both purchased, it is likely that different segments want the features for different reasons and you'll have to dig into who purchased the specific features to see what is motivating the purchases. If you can't discern what your customers want, you'll need to leverage these results into more research, armed with the knowledge that you know you need to explore these specific features in greater detail.

Avoid selling features that you're not going to put into the product even if customers buy them. That's intentionally misleading and will only frustrate customers.

Buy a Feature introduces an additional role to your team: *feature retailer.* The feature retailer is responsible for managing the selling of features to attendees. This person manages the purchase of features, keeping track of who purchased what feature. You will need one feature retailer and one observer per group of customers playing the game. For small numbers of customer groups—typically less than three—the facilitator can play the role of the feature retailer for one group of customers. For larger groups of customers, the facilitator needs to be available to work across the groups, answering the questions that will surface from the feature retailers as they are playing the game.

Materials

- ☐ List of possible, planned, or hypothetical features and descriptions of the same, with prices for each one.

- ☐ Play money. As described earlier, consider creating your own. Alternatively, you can use Monopoly money, which you can purchase online at stores such as www.areyougame.com, or purchase play money at stores that sell teaching supplies.

Playing the Game

When introducing this game, the facilitator should stress that it is a game and that there is no promise that the features purchased during the game will actually appear in a future product.

The feature retailers have special responsibilities to ensure that the game produces the most accurate representations of customer desires. They should not steer, guide, recommend, nor otherwise try to motivate customers to purchase certain features. They should not change the price of a feature. They should be able to fully explain each feature, so it is best if the feature retailer is a member of the product team. The feature retailer must keep in mind that the personal favorite feature of any given member of the team may not be purchased, and customers may not spend all their money.

Glenn Grossman of Ticketmaster prepared a simple tracking spreadsheet to keep track of which customer purchased what feature (see Table 2.3). When the game was done, the spreadsheet automatically produced statistics as to which features were purchased, which customers participated in the purchase, and so forth. It also provides a convenient place for the feature retailer to record observations about the interactions among participants.

Create a tracking sheet and print it for use during the game. Because it is fairly common for participants to ask to return a feature when negotiations become complex, use a pencil when writing items in your tracking sheet. To help customers keep track of what the group has purchased, consider printing the tracking table as a large poster and having your helper write the results on the poster. When finished, transcribe your results back into the spreadsheet and use it to process game results.

Resist the temptation to give more money to customers who run out and ask for more, because it defeats the purpose of the exercise. When money is free, so are the features.

PROCESSING THE RESULTS

Collect the list of features purchased by each group of customers as a single group, taking care to keep track of which customers were playing the game. Merge the purchased features into a single list and sort them based on how many groups of customers purchased the feature. The features purchased by more than one group of customers should receive the highest consideration for inclusion into your product. Correlate purchases with observations about the interactions with customers who purchased the features; they can provide insight into marketing messages for key segments.

Table 2.3   Tracking Sheet for Customer Purchases

	Customer	Feature 1	Feature 2	...	Feature n-1	Feature n
	Price	34	21	2	4	4
1	<customer name>					
2	<customer name>					
3	<customer name>					
4						
5						
6						
7						
8						
	Subtotal					

How I Can Use Buy a Feature

_____

_____

_____

_____

_____

_____

_____

_____

_____

_____

_____

_____

_____

_____

_____

_____

_____

_____

Start Your Day

Understand When and How Your Customer Uses Your Product

Products might seem static, but they're not. Well, at least not like you might think. The product may be static, but our relationship to the product isn't. It changes based on how we use it. And how we use a product changes based on lots of factors, including our age, experience with this product or other similar products, or even our location. One of the biggest modifiers of *how* we use a product is *when* we use it. By focusing on the when, you'll get better insights into the how.

Consider that the insulated mug that keeps your coffee hot in the morning keeps your juice cold in the afternoon. Chances are pretty good that you use your financial planning software differently when you review your monthly budget versus when you prepare your taxes. You may rely on your favorite email/scheduling program to help you start your day by planning it and to help you end your day by tracking which "to-dos" actually got done.

The Game

On preprinted, poster-sized calendars or on a simple timeline drawn on a large sheet of paper, ask your customers to describe the daily, weekly, monthly, and yearly events that are related to their use of your product. Ask them to describe events in time frames appropriate for your product—beginnings and ends of days or weeks, recurring events such as birthdays, one-time events such as installing a new software system, special events that are unique to an industry or sector (like a conference), or days in which everything goes horribly wrong and they're looking for help. While they're doing this, be alert for how your product helps, or hinders, their day.

Open-Ended Exploration

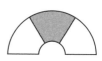

Time Frame of Action

Scalability

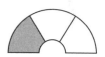

Customer Preparation

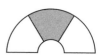

Market Preparation

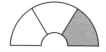

Physical Preparation

FIGURE 2.13 Playing Start Your Day

Why It Works

When we ask customers something about our product, they usually respond to our question based on their most recent experiences. Unfortunately, this creates a skewed view of how a product works throughout its natural life cycle. By explicitly asking your customers the *when* of using a product, you'll substantially increase your ability to understand the *how* to make it better.

More generally, *Start Your Day* is about exploring different contexts in which your customers use your product. In the game, you vary the time context. As you do this, pay attention to how other contexts change. For example, you might find that your customer uses your email/scheduling program at the beginning of the day from their home office and at the end of the day from their work office. These locations are quite different, and understanding how they differ provides you with substantial insight into the problems your customer is trying to solve. This understanding, in turn, leads to innovations.

You can enhance this game by varying other aspects of product use and then exploring these effects with your customers while they are working on their calendars. Suppose, for example, that you were a manufacturer of binoculars. In addition to posting calendars, you could post the following:

- Pictures of different locations—Ask customers to tell you how they use binoculars at sporting events, at the opera, at the park, at the beach, and in the woods.

- Pictures of situations with varying amounts of ambient light—Ask customers to tell you how they use binoculars in conditions of bright sunlight, normal light, dawn, dusk, and in the middle of the night.

- Pictures of people in different physical and/or emotional states—Ask customers to tell you how they use binoculars when they are carrying other things, such as during a hiking trip, when they are tired (after a long day of hiking), or when they're excited (perhaps because they have just glimpsed the rare ruby-throated humming bird).

The good news is that when you've made the time context explicit, it is relatively easy to vary other things and get very useful information.

Preparing for the Game

Selecting the customers who will produce the best results is a common theme throughout the book. In this game, it helps to consider how different customers may be affected by time and then select customers who fit different time profiles. For example, if you're interested in how school schedules impact a parent's use of your product, you may want to include parents who send their children to public schools, parents who send their children to private schools, parents who home school their children, and parents who employ tutors or nannies. Each of these schooling options creates different time demands on parents.

This also means that you must focus your efforts on producing calendars that are specific to the question you're asking. If you're asking customers about their child care needs, you might find that a poster of the school year is the most useful representation of time. If you're asking about their use of athletic gear, you need to match the calendars to the sport.

Make certain that you also hang several blank sheets of paper. Although our use of a product or service is influenced by time, it is also influenced by events. By allowing your customers to record and share key events that motivate or adjust their use of your product, you'll gain greater, richer understanding into their underlying needs.

Give each participant a different colored pen so that you can keep track of which customer made what comment on the posters. If you have more than one person from the same company or family participating, consider giving each of them different colored pens so that you can track each person's contributions.

Give customers a simple way to agree with what other customers say they do with your products. My favorite approach for signaling agreement is to let customers place a brightly colored sticker, such as a gold star or a word like "Yeah" or "Excellent," next to something that someone else has written. Stickers keep the mood fun, and the different words that customers choose provide you with additional opportunities to ask them specific questions regarding why they chose that particular word to signify agreement.

Materials

❑ Calendars in both normal and large print format. Consider the following time formats:

- Day-by-Hour (all 24)
- Week-by-Day
- Monthly
- Year-by-Month
- Year-by-Quarter
- Seasons
- Holidays

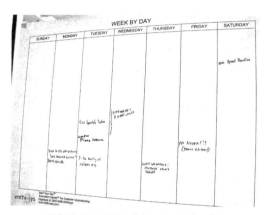

FIGURE 2.14 Week-by-Day Calendar

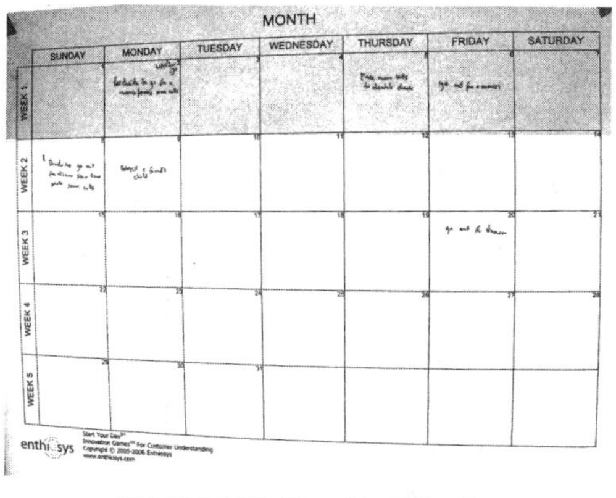

FIGURE 2.15 Monthly Calendar

Market Events and Market Rhythms

Every market is governed by one-time and recurring events. As you prepare for *Start Your Day*, consider how you can use market events and market rhythms to better understand your customers. To illustrate, several years ago I tried to start a company to promote financial literacy for children and young adults through specially designed parent-controlled financial services. The company never got off the ground, but the research was fascinating. In this case, I found capturing events that signify increasing financial literacy, such as a child's first purchase or a young adult's first job, as "Life Firsts" helpful. The recurring events mapped into the rhythms of American culture that are present every year, but change based on age. There is quite a difference in how a 10-year-old and 16-year-old boy approaches Valentine's day and Halloween. You may be able to leverage this approach in planning

for your use of the game: What are the "Product Firsts" that your customers have in relation to your product and the goals that they are trying to accomplish when using your product? What are recurring rhythms that your customers must address? How does your product help or hinder their efforts? The Internet is a treasure trove of calendar-related information, and you should not have a problem finding good inspiration and supporting information for your game.

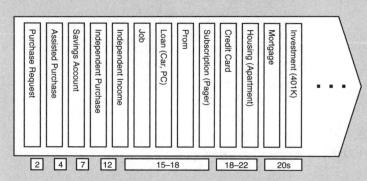

FIGURE 2.16 Life Firsts—Age of Financial Decisions

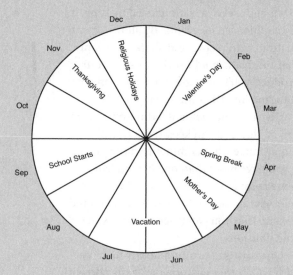

FIGURE 2.17 Partial List of American Holiday Rhythms

PLAYING THE GAME

Customers often need a bit of prompting with this exercise. You can help them by giving them a warm-up exercise, such as asking them how they use gardening equipment at different times of the year. Do they use the garden hose to wash their car, water their lawn, or add water to their children's sand box? You can also help them by preparing timelines and/or events that are appropriate for your product.

After you have given customers a few minutes to think about how they use your product, ask them to take a walk around the room and look at each of the calendars that you've printed out in poster format. This will give them a chance to consider the different time frames that you have chosen.

Month

Season

Week by Day   Day by Hour

Participants in Start Your Day walk around the room, adding to the calendars as the game is played.

FIGURE 2.18 Playing Start Your Day

After customers start writing down how they use your product or service, encourage them to take several passes through the calendars. Looking at how other customers have used your product will almost certainly help them remember similar experiences of their own.

When all customers have finished writing their entries on the posters, the facilitator announces a break of about 15 minutes. During the break, the photographer should take a set of photos of the final customer entries. After customers return, the facilitator should review the entries, confirming the results and engaging participants in a discussion about unusual or confusing entries. The facilitator may add clarifying notes to what is written, ideally using a 3"×5" or 5"×8" index card

placed next to the original customer entry; this allows you to retain the original entry as well as the clarifying note. When finished, the facilitator should thank participants and end the game, and the photographer should take one final set of photos of the customer entries along with any of the facilitator's notes.

PROCESSING THE RESULTS

Using the original materials and photos, transcribe every customer entry into a spreadsheet that is organized by the same time frame in which the comment was made, keeping track of which customer made each entry, along with any clarifying text from the participant discussion. This means that if you used three calendars during the game, one based on a single day, another on a month, and a third on an entire year, you should have at least three spreadsheets organized around the same time frames. You might be tempted to put each entry into a single spreadsheet, but this approach often fails to match customers' perceptions of time.

Associate additional attributes with each entry so that you can better understand patterns and trends. Attributes that you may find useful and what you can do with them include the following:

- The degree to which this is the intended use of your product, ranging from a simple yes/no to a scale from 1 to 3 or 1 to 5. A product that has many unintended uses can be the most challenging to understand. On one hand, the product may be selling well because of these unintended uses, which tends to make people happy because market share and profits are good. But this unintended result is rarely what you want. One problem is that the real market need, and the one that motivated the creation of the product in the first place, is left unanswered. Another problem is that if the product is selling well based on unintended use, what might happen if the company actually identified the right target market and promoted the product to them? Could sales double or triple? Keep in mind that not all unintended uses of a product represent improper design. Indeed, a few unintended uses are usually a benefit, as they help the product team identify new opportunities. Finally, note that unintended uses include things that might appear normal at the surface but upon closer inspection reveal a novel or unintended use. For example, consider the number of people who keep track of "to do" items by adding "appointments" to their calendars.

- The degree to which your team was surprised by this use of your product, again using a simple "yes/no" or more complex numeric scale. The greater the surprise, the greater the opportunity for identifying and/or marketing your product to a new set of customers or for increasing use of your product by existing customers.

- Your customers' perceptions of how easy it was to use your product to accomplish the task they described. Tasks that your product supports should be retained. Tasks that are difficult to accomplish are clear opportunities for improvement.

- The number of customers who indicated they used the product in a similar manner; consensus strengthens the points described previously.

How I Can Use Start Your Day

Show and Tell

Identify the Most Important Artifacts Created by Your Product

Much like a child excitedly sharing his most prized possession at school during show-and-tell, customers are often equally excited about the results that they can produce with your product, and they'll tell you all about it—if you let them. In the process, you'll gain new insights into what really matters.

THE GAME

Ask your customers to bring examples of artifacts created or modified by your product or service. Ask them to tell you why these artifacts are important and when and how they're used. For example, if your product is a software system to manage invoices, ask them to show you the invoices, reports, or spreadsheets that they've created through using your product. If you make running shoes, ask your customers to bring you several pairs of worn shoes and tell you about all their runs.

Pay careful attention to anything that surprises you. What did you expect customers to create or modify that they have ignored? What things can you do with your product or service that aren't used? What was used in unexpected ways? What do these tell you?

WHY IT WORKS

Countless studies have demonstrated something that great managers have known for a long time—most people want to do a good job. It doesn't really matter if the person is a barber, a construction worker, an accountant, or a software developer. All want to demonstrate their special skills.[5] *Show and Tell* works by giving your customers a chance to dip into a deeply felt human emotion to show you when and how they are using your product to do their best. By telling you how they are doing the best they can, they will also be telling you how you can help them do it better.

PREPARING FOR THE GAME

Show and Tell requires a lot of work from your customers to prepare for the game. Do everything you can to make this easy for them. Give them detailed instructions on what to bring and plenty of time to prepare the materials. Ask them in advance if you can keep whatever they bring so they aren't surprised during the game. One way to do this is to offer a new product in exchange for the old product.

There are times when customers will want to bring examples that are private or that contain sensitive information. In this case, offer a private audience with just you and your customer to review these private objects. You won't gain the benefit of other customers' comments and reactions, but you will gain a more complete and thorough understanding of how your customers use your products and services.

5. Perhaps a parent doesn't want to show special skill in changing a diaper, but they certainly want to do a good job!

Open-Ended Exploration

Time Frame of Action

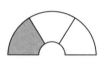

Scalability

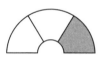

Customer Preparation

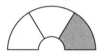

Market Preparation

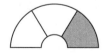

Physical Preparation

When playing this game with multiple customers, be certain to find a way to identify which customer provided which artifact. If you're having trouble with this, ask your customers to sign or personalize what they bring after they've finished presenting.

You need to create and bring a full set of materials created by your product because your customers will usually bring only the subset of materials that they actually use. For example, suppose your product is a software program that generates 40 standard reports. Chances are good that some reports will be perceived as more useful than others, and your customer will typically bring only the subset of reports that they normally use. By bringing a standard set of all of your reports, you'll also gain the advantage of asking them to comment about what they *don't* use.

Although this game is best played with a small group of customers who can ask questions and elaborate further on what is being presented (and therefore help you learn more

about how your product is used), it is a great game to run during a single customer visit.

Products that don't produce much in the way of directly tangible results are not good candidates for this game. Business-oriented software systems that produce various reports, charts, and graphs are a good choice for this game. Software that doesn't produce much in tangible results, such as games or the embedded software that controls your microwave oven or antilock brakes, are not. Many items in the physical works are also not good choices for this game. Chairs are used for sitting, cups for drinking, and tape for holding things to walls. If you want to learn more about how customers use these products, consider *Me and My Shadow* or *The Apprentice*.

Materials

❏ Sample copy of "standard" things created by your product or service

---

Anything You Can Do with a Single Customer Is Likely to be More Interesting with Multiple Customers

Like most Innovation Games, *Show and Tell* is a game that you can play with a single customer. For example, suppose that you're a vendor of high-end machining equipment and you're visiting your customer to upgrade their control software. During the trip, it is very natural to play *Show and Tell* and learn more about how they use your products and services. Learning more about your customers is always a good thing and should be encouraged.

However, a key tenet of the design of the games is that anything you can do with a single customer is likely to be more interesting with multiple customers present. Play *Show and Tell* with a customer and you'll learn how one customer uses your product. Play *Show and Tell* with other customers present and you'll not

only learn how they use your product, you'll learn how other customers react to the presentation. You'll be able to observe rich conversations where customers question, challenge, extend, and modify product usage, often sharing best practices, heuristics, and "never do this" advice. Perhaps more importantly, your customers will do the questioning, which can itself be a source of rich insight. What questions do they ask? Why did they ask these questions?

Ultimately, it is not a question of the right or wrong way to engage your customer. Instead, it is about the degree to which you can gain powerful insights into customer needs, and you should feel comfortable using any number of customers that you can to realize this goal.

Playing the Game

Take photos of all artifacts before, during, and after the game so that you can track any changes made to the artifacts during the game.

It is much more powerful to convince a skeptical product team that changes are needed when your customer presents their ideas in their own words. To make this easier, encourage your customers to bring extra copies of artifacts created by your system so that you, and they, can edit, annotate, or mark up these artifacts as they wish (use markers, scissors, glue, tape, paper, transparencies, and so on). If the artifacts are expensive to produce, such as when your system helps make teddy bears, sneakers, or portable MP3 players, offer to reimburse your client for artifacts you take with you or ask them to bring mock-ups or even photos.

How I Can Use Show and Tell

_____

_____

_____

_____

_____

_____

_____

_____

Processing the Results

Organize your results into the following categories and analyze them as follows:

- Artifacts created or modified in normal/expected ways. Compare these with your future development plans to ensure that you are continuing to support the normal use of your product. As the old saying goes, "If it ain't broken, don't fix it."

- Artifacts created or modified in surprising ways. These are your greatest areas of opportunity to learn from your customers how your product can be extended to meet their needs or tap new markets.

- Artifacts not created or used. These represent areas in which your total offering can be improved or simplified. For example, it could be that your product is just fine but your education and/or reference manuals are lousy. Alternatively, it could mean that your product is over engineered and that features can be removed.

Using Other Innovation Games with Show and Tell

Playing _Show and Tell_ can be more fun, and produce even more interesting results, when you leverage other Innovation Games to create a more compelling experience. For example,

- Leverage _Product Box_ and bring markers, pens, and other things that your customers can use to mark up existing artifacts, telling you about what they've done and selling you on their new creations.

- Leverage _Start Your Day_ and ask customers to show and tell you about how they use your product during different times of the day, week, month, or year.

- Leverage _Remember the Future_ to help your customer envision how the current artifacts could be made more useful.

As you become comfortable with all of the games, you'll find that you can leverage the concepts behind one game with other games.

Me and My Shadow

Identify Your Customers' Hidden Needs

Designers have a wealth of ideas on how their products can and should be used. These idealized notions keep competitors and quality assurance people in business, as designers never seem to include the idea that a cell phone makes a great door stop, or that a remote controlled toy dump truck is the best way to move your keys, wallet, and the TV remote control across the room after you've had knee surgery, or that the best way to soothe a crying baby is to put them on top of the washer or dryer.[6] Of course, few of your customers will remember to tell you about these experiences. To learn about them, you need to watch your customers use your product on *their* terms, not yours.

THE GAME

Shadow your customers while they use your product or service. Literally. Sit or stand next to them and watch what they do. Periodically ask them, "Why are you doing that?" and "What are you thinking?" Take along a camera and make photos of key activities and the context in which work is accomplished. Ask for copies of important artifacts created or used by your customers while they are doing the work. Bring along other customers and use them as interpreters to explain what a customer is doing, help you ask clarifying questions as to why the customer is doing things this way. During the game, ask your other customers to share whether they do

things the same way with the person you're observing, and watch how your customers explore and even debate the various approaches they bring to using your products and services.

Me and My Shadow differs from *The Apprentice* in that *Me and My Shadow* focuses on observation and *The Apprentice* focuses on experience.

WHY IT WORKS

This technique is one of many that falls under the broad category of *ethnographic research*. Ethnographic research is an incredibly powerful way of understanding your customer, but it comes with a catch: it is hard to observe your customer in such a way that your observations don't change how they work. It's kind of like the Heisenberg Uncertainty Principle[7] applied to people instead of quantum particles. That's why the name of this game emphasizes thinking of yourself as a shadow, so that you can minimize any negative interactions caused by your observations.

Sophisticated applications of this technique are based on specially selected customers being asked to perform activities while being studied in specially constructed observation rooms. Although this can be an extraordinary way to uncover hidden

Open-Ended Exploration

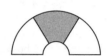

Time Frame of Action

Scalability

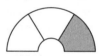

Customer Preparation

Market Preparation

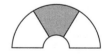

Physical Preparation

---

6. As a parent of four wonderful children, I'm still surprised that some clever inventor hasn't built a car seat harness for a washing machine.

7. The Heisenberg Uncertainty Principle was discovered by the physicist Werner Heisenberg in 1927. Among other things, it states that observing (measuring) a particle changes it. This is similar to what happens when you observe people: they tend to change their behavior.

requirements, the process is both expensive because of the special room charges and time consuming, and the setting tends to be artificial. *Me and My Shadow* works best when you can observe your customers in their native habitat (with native guides in tow).

Preparing for the Game

Consider the working context of your customer in preparing for this game. You may need special preparations or approvals because of safety, privacy, security, or related factors. Addressing these items early in the planning process will make certain that you have time to handle all the necessary details before playing the game. A detailed examination of these factors is beyond the scope of this book because laws governing this behavior vary considerably by country.

This game often takes longer than other games. Depending on the location of your customers and the factors mentioned above, it may also cost more money.

Me and My Shadow can be used anytime, but you'll obtain the best results when you try this technique on nontraditional customer segments. To illustrate, consider segmenting your customers by experience: new customers, customers who have used your product for one month, six months, and one year or more. Alternatively, try segmenting your customers based on perceived motivation: those who want to use your product, those who are indifferent about using your product, and those who don't want to use your product but cannot find or justify an alternative, and in rare cases, those who may be forced to use your product. Although you

may not be able to change their motivation for using your product, you will find that you develop different insights from each group.

Although you'll try your best to miss nothing, chances are pretty good that you'll miss a lot of things. That's understandable, because there is often so much to see that it is hard to know what to observe. Do the best that you can and don't expect that to be perfect. Take comfort in the knowledge that making the commitment to develop customer understanding using these games will put you ahead of your competition.

As you prepare to play the game, consider exactly who will join you at the customer site. You probably won't need a helper or a facilitator. You will still need observers and a photographer. Inquire about any security policies because you may have to obtain special badges or access permissions for your team. You may also need special permission to bring along cameras.

Materials

❑ Notepads or notebooks
❑ Recording devices appropriate to the task at hand as approved by your customer

Playing the Game

Arrive early and be respectful of the cultural norms of your customers, including the way that they dress. Don't force them to immediately use your product. Instead, establish a rapport and let your customer control the pace at which the visit unfolds. You'll get your chance to observe your customer. Honor all requests to stop making observations or to leave the room, especially when concern

To Video or Not Video

You may think that capturing participants on a video camera for subsequent review is the best way to play this game. Although a record of behavior can be compelling, I recommend against this for a variety of reasons:

- Observers tend to become sloppy in their observations when they think they can go back and watch a video tape.

- Unlike the role of the Bad Wedding Photographer, in which lots of photos take the place of a few high quality photos, video needs to be more professionally obtained. The need for greater degrees of professionalism (that is, making certain the camera isn't jiggled, providing adequate light, ensuring that audio levels are correct, and so forth) substantially increases costs.

- The professional aspect of the video tends to highlight the fact that participants are being watched, which often causes them to change their behavior. This can be contrasted with the Bad Wedding Photographer, as many times participants forget that they're being photographed (especially when a lot of photographs are taken and they are not asked to pose for the camera).

- There are often complex legal issues associated with videotaping subjects, especially in Europe, and EMEA.

- It takes between 5 and 10 hours (and some say longer) to review one hour of video. In other words, video review is a slow, expensive process. More importantly, in many cases it does not produce a materially better result than recording your impressions in real time and then reviewing your results as a team.

Whereas videotaping customers usually creates more problems than it is worth, carefully selected photographs can be your best friend. By focusing on the results of the work, you can record the most essential elements of the work and avoid many, if not all, of the issues (especially legal issues). If you really think that video is superior to photographs, consider that in the real estate market, prospective buyers tend to prefer a few well-chosen photos (which just about anyone can take with high quality) to a video walkthrough.

There are times when even I will concede that a video record is the most powerful way of communicating your observations. A skeptical product team who just can't believe that their product is hard to use can be convinced a redesign is required when they observe customers struggling to accomplish basic tasks. If you feel that you simply must use video to accomplish your goals, then do so, but keep in mind the potential land mines discussed earlier.

or fear is expressed ("You're not going to tell my boss that I'm not sure how to operate all features of this machine, are you?").

In most Innovation Games, observers record observations on 5"×8" cards, one observation per card. In this game it is better to bring along a simple notepad or notebook and jot down the details you think are necessary. I prefer unlined paper so that I can make quick sketches. Others prefer graph paper. As you make your observations, record the time, location, and customers involved. If it helps, bring along a voice recorder and record your observations.

As soon as you finish with your customer, find a private location and *immediately* write down everything that you can remember. The longer you delay, the more that you risk forgetting. While you're recording your observations, try to avoid making evaluations. That comes later, during the normal phase of observer note processing. In this phase you should simply focus on your perceptions and observations.

Here are some of the things you may want to capture in your observations:

- The people who interact with your customer.

- The products and services that they use at the same time they are using your products or services.

- Utterances, body language, or facial expressions that give insight into their emotions as they use your products or services.

- The physical environment and larger context of their workspace.

- Your own feelings and reactions to what is going on.

Processing the Results

Organize a meeting of everyone who visited or observed customers. It is best if everyone can attend this meeting in person (not a teleconference). Hand each person a stack of 5"×8" note cards and masking tape or large sticky notes and ask them to transcribe their observations onto these cards, one per card. When they have finished, ask them to tape each card to the wall. Review each observation, grouping them into meaningful patterns. Discuss the patterns, capturing any meta-observations (observations about the patterns and/or the observations) as new observations. Next, do the following:

1. Transcribe all observations into a spreadsheet, with one observation in each row.

2. Assess each observation along the following dimensions:

   - Novelty—The degree to which the observation indicates a novel or unintended use of the product.

   - Performance gap—The degree to which the observation indicates a performance gap between desired and actual performance. Large gaps mean large problems.

   - New opportunity—The degree to which the observation indicates a new opportunity for solving a customer problem.

   For example, suppose you make various tools for home gardening and you decide to watch how home gardeners use these tools. You might observe that a home gardener forms a "pouch" with their shirt to hold vegetables they pick from their garden. If you or your team have never seen this before, you might rank it as highly novel, with no relationship to your existing tools, and a strong new opportunity for a new solution that would help gardeners hold the vegetables that they pick (like a special gardening shirt with big pouches).

How I Can Use Me and My Shadow

_____

_____

_____

_____

_____

_____

_____

_____

_____

_____

_____

_____

_____

_____

_____

_____

_____

_____

Give Them a Hot Tub

Use Outrageous Features to Discover Hidden Breakthroughs

Brainstorming is an attempt to leverage the creative power of a group of people who are trying to solve a problem by encouraging them to come up with as many different ideas as possible. Then the ideas are evaluated and one or more are selected as potential candidates for solving the problem, presumably in an innovative way.

When brainstorming is done well, it can be effective in generating breakthroughs. Consider, though, that traditional approaches to brainstorming are biased toward internal groups of people. That's okay, but I've found that the *real* breakthroughs come when you work directly with customers. So, instead of generating and evaluating your own "crazy" ideas, the *Give Them a Hot Tub* game encourages you to generate your crazy ideas and let your customers determine just how crazy those ideas really are!

THE GAME

Write several features on note cards, one feature per card. Include several outrageous features. For example, if you're making a portable MP3 player, try adding features like "heats coffee," "cracks concrete," or "conditions dog hair." If you're making a system that manages payroll, try adding features like "plans family reunions" or "refinishes wooden floors." If you're building an office building, add a hot tub in the lobby. What happens when a customer uncovers one of these outrageous features?

WHY IT WORKS

An outrageous feature induces cognitive dissonance. That's fancy language for saying that an outrageous feature makes customers uncomfortable. So, they work (mentally) to get rid of the discomfort. The most common ways to deal with the discomfort are rejecting the feature outright, pretending that the feature was never really discussed, or transforming the "outrageous" feature into something that isn't so outrageous. The magic happens during these transformations—they are the things that can create breakthroughs in the product.

This game is useful if you need to build products that operate in various "extreme" environments, because you typically can't easily simulate or access the extreme environment. Examples of extreme environments include those that are physically demanding or dangerous or those where the risk of human, societal, or financial damage is high should a failure occur. In these situations, the *Give Them a Hot Tub* game enables you to safely explore potential solutions for extreme environments.

PREPARING FOR THE GAME

You'll need at least two preparation meetings to generate your features. The first meeting is a warm-up meeting where you generate your initial list of outrageous features. This shouldn't take long—about an hour. Start the process by generating a list of features. Some should be normal and could be taken from your existing list of features. Some should be

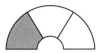

Open-Ended Exploration

Time Frame of Action

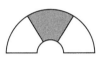

Scalability

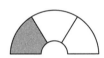

Customer Preparation

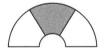

Market Preparation

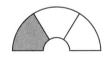

Physical Preparation

outrageous and will probably require a bit of creativity on the part of your product team. Take a few days' break and then meet again to revise this initial set of features. The break will give your subconscious mind time to become more comfortable with the process, with the result being a richer and more diverse set of normal-to-outrageous features. The result of these two meetings will be a list of potential features, some of which are going to be outrageous.

The biggest preparation challenge when playing this game is creating features that are extreme enough to cause cognitive dissonance, yet not so extreme as to force customers to reject the game. There is no easy way to do this, which is why you'll need at least two preparation meetings for this exercise. For example, although I think a fountain pen with a nib that can cut glass is a bit outrageous, I find myself trying to transform this idea into something useful ("Hey, if it can cut glass, that means it should last a long time, right?") However, I can't possibly imagine using a fountain pen to launch a satellite into a geosynchronous earth orbit. Keep in mind that your goal isn't to generate some perfect set of easily explainable plausible features.

Materials

There are no special materials for this game.

PLAYING THE GAME

This game works best when the facilitator lets customers know that during the game they will be asked to comment on a variety of features, some of which they might consider "funny" or "outrageous." Doing so will slightly reduce the degree of cognitive dissonance customers experience, because they have been preconditioned, but often helps to increase the number of ideas that they attempt to transform because they are more aligned with the fun element of the game.

The facilitator presents each feature to customers and invites them to respond in one of three ways:

- Accept the feature as is with no changes.
- Reject the feature outright as something they don't want.
- Transform the feature into a new feature that is something that they do want.

Customers will often transform outrageous features into an existing feature with a more desirable set of attributes, as I did when I transformed the fountain pen that could cut glass into a fountain pen with a stronger and/or longer lasting nib. This process might give you understanding into my desire for a stronger and/or longer lasting nib, but it doesn't give you sufficient insight into the underlying problem or need that is driving this transformation. To really understand your customers, you're going to have to ask them to explain their transformations. In my case, you would find that although I once owned a fountain pen, a colleague borrowed it and dropped it on the floor, irreparably damaging the nib.

PROCESSING THE RESULTS

The key element in processing the results is the notes from your observers, who were watching your customers during the game and recording how they transformed certain features into something useful. Capture both the initial outrageous feature and how this feature was ultimately transformed.

As described earlier, consider carefully whether your customer is actually requesting a new feature or if they are transforming the outrageous feature into an enhanced attribute of an existing feature. These desires for enhancements must be prioritized against your existing near- and long-term product development plans.

How I Can Use Give Them a Hot Tub

The Apprentice

Create Empathy for the Customer Experience

When you understand your customers' needs so well that you can envision solutions to problems they may not realize they have, you are well on your path to creating innovative products and services. This game, which helps create empathy for the customer, allows you to take the path that leads to innovation with your customer at your side.

The Game

Ask your development team to perform the "work" of the system that they are building. If they're creating a new masking tape for painters, ask them to work with real painters, using the masking tape in the field. If they're creating a new professional oven, ask them to cook meals with a professional chef—not in a classroom, but in a real restaurant, where they have to experience the actual challenges of creating meals. If they're building workflow management software for furniture delivery people, have them deliver furniture. They will gain direct knowledge of the problems customers face and empathy for how hard it may be to solve them.

Warning! Play this game with some common sense! This game is not recommended for such things as Formula One race car driving, neurosurgery, or high-explosives research.

Why It Works

Product designers who empathize with their customers create better solutions. For some people, this empathy comes naturally. For others, it is harder. *The Apprentice* provides members of your product team with the opportunity to create the empathy that they need to create innovative products and services. As a bonus, it also provides them with a wealth of concrete, direct experience that they can use during the product development process.

Preparing for the Game

Whereas most of the games can be played in a few hours, this one usually takes longer. Two or three days is common, but don't be alarmed if this technique takes as long as a week of customer interaction spread out over one to two weeks of calendar time. Part of the reason for this is that you'll want to leverage the concepts behind *Start Your Day* and try doing your customer's job at different times of the day. You'll also need a little extra time to move behind just the bare basics of a job. It doesn't take too long to replace the brake pads on a mountain bike. It takes quite a bit longer to replace the brake assembly. It takes even longer to replace the brake assembly on a mountain bike, a street bike, and a racing bike. Let your market experience guide how long you'll need to be an apprentice to gain an appreciation for the tasks they are trying to accomplish. Use this feedback to help you justify to your superiors the amount of time you'll need to play the game.

When selecting customers for this game, make certain that you let them know that they will be working with novices, and that these novices will be asking lots of questions about how they do their jobs. Ultimately, if possible, the apprentices will actually be performing their jobs.

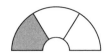

Open-Ended Exploration

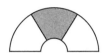

Time Frame of Action

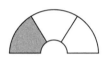

Scalability

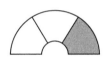

Customer Preparation

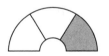

Market Preparation

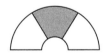

Physical Preparation

Materials

As dictated by the job you and/or your team is performing.

PLAYING THE GAME

Start by confirming that your apprentices are appropriately physically and mentally prepared for the task.

Remind your apprentices to ask *lots* of questions during the game. It is the best way for them to learn from their experiences.

Encourage your apprentices to maintain a notebook or diary of their experiences. During the game, meet daily for 20 to 30 minutes to review their most important discoveries and capture how their understanding of the product that they need to create is changing based on their experiences. When finished, review each day's insights and consolidate them into a larger document. Note that you'll often discard earlier observations in favor of later observations, when your team has a more genuine understanding of the task. Consider inviting your customers to attend these review meetings, so that they can further work with your team to clarify any misconceptions about the job.

PROCESSING THE RESULTS

As you prepare to process your findings, keep in mind that playing *The Apprentice* game doesn't always turn up the need for new features or changes to your product; sometimes you will find your product is just fine the way it is. With that as a preamble, here is a means for processing the results from this game.

We'll Just Keep Going Until You Actually Care About Your Customer

This game is especially effective when you suspect that the product team doesn't care enough about the people using the product. To illustrate, many years ago I was asked to lead a group of software developers who were charged with creating a new data entry system. Unfortunately, this particular group of developers exhibited some of the most blatant negative stereotypes we associate with "geeks"—insensitive, surly, and downright rude to the data entry personnel who they felt were "beneath them." To reset their thinking, I asked them to play this game by performing the jobs of the data entry operators (the developers would probably tell you I forced them to play the game).

During the first few days, the bulk of their complaints were muttered profanities referencing my draconian management practices. After a few more days, the bulk of their complaints were directed toward the genuinely poorly designed existing system. After a few more days, when the bulk of their complaints became grumblings for me to allow them to "fix the terrible problems that aren't letting those poor data entry operators do a good job," I knew that they had finally developed some genuine empathy for the customer and were ready to begin working on the new system.

I've since learned that great product managers just about always use their products—no matter what industry they work in.

Schedule a meeting of everyone who played the game. Ask people who are coming to the meeting to review their experience notebook and bring their most important observations and learnings to the meeting. Then, using a process similar to that described in *Me and My Shadow*, give each person a stack of 5"×8" note cards and ask them to transcribe their observations onto these cards, one per card. When finished, ask them to tape each card to the wall. Review each observation, grouping them into meaningful patterns. Discuss the patterns, capturing any meta-observations (observations about the patterns and/or the observations) as new observations.

After the meeting, do the following:

1. Transcribe all observations into a spreadsheet, with one observation in each row.

2. Assess each observation along the following dimensions:

- Performance gap—The degree to which the observation indicates a performance gap between desired and actual performance. Large gaps mean large problems.

- New opportunity—The degree to which the observation indicates a new opportunity for solving a customer problem.

- Product Is Fine But...—The degree to which the observation indicates a problem in another component of your total solution. Be vigilant for observations that indicate problems with training materials, configuration of the system, and so forth.

- Solution—It is inevitable that some of the observations will actually be solutions to problems encountered in the team. That's okay, just record them as such.

HOW I CAN USE THE APPRENTICE

_____

_____

_____

_____

_____

_____

_____

The Apprentice Is Not Dogfooding

Dogfooding means that a company uses the products it makes. This is a great idea, for a number of reasons (see the entry in Wikipedia for the details). However, *The Apprentice* is not Dogfooding. One reason is that there are many times when the product team can't Dogfood, such as when they're making a component that is a part of another product or creating products for a business or professional context that does not match their own. An even more important reason, and the key point of differentiation between *The Apprentice* and Dogfooding, is that when you're Dogfooding you're doing your job using your product. In *The Apprentice*, you're putting yourself into your customers' environment, doing their job, in their context, with your product and any other related products. The end result is a deeper and more empathetic understanding of the challenges your customer faces and how your product helps—or hinders—their work.

20/20 Vision

Understand Customer Priorities

Effective product teams not only understand which set of features must be present to justify a release, they have carefully enumerated the ranking of each.[8] They know which is "number one," which is "number two." They know which set of stakeholders care the most about number one, which care the most about number two, and so on. They also know that different market segments may not agree among these rankings, so they seek to understand differences among the market segments. The most effective product teams take this even further and can demonstrate how their prioritization supports larger business priorities (and when the business priorities aren't clear, these teams clarify them!). The challenge is understanding the underlying qualitative motivations to market-driven priorities.

THE GAME

When you're getting fitted for glasses, your optometrist will often ask you to compare two potential lenses by alternately showing each of them ("which of these lenses is better—number one or number two?"). Although it may take some time, eventually you'll settle on the set of lenses that are best for your eyes. You can use a variant of this approach to help your customers see which

---

8. Note: Effective products teams do *not* try to justify every possible feature for all releases at once—just the set of features needed for the next release of their product (and perhaps a few more). Effective product teams do *not* spend the same amount of time prioritizing every feature. Some features are just too inconsequential to justify the effort.

priorities are best for them, as customers often have trouble "seeing" which features are the highest priority, especially if you're asking them to compare several features at the same time.

Start by writing one feature each on large index cards. Shuffle the pile and put them face down. Take the first one from the top of the pile and put it on the wall. Take the next one and ask your customers if it is more or less important than the one on the wall. If it is more important, place it higher. If it is less important, put it lower. Avoid placing the item at the same level; try hard to rank each feature. Repeat this process with all your feature cards, and you'll develop 20/20 vision for what your market really wants.

WHY IT WORKS

Although just about every customer knows that they can't have everything they want in a product, they also know that, until you work with them to prioritize features, they have the upper hand in asking you for whatever they want. Perhaps more importantly, features of complex products are interrelated, and the product design and development team often faces a continuum of possible solutions that could meet customer needs. Asking your customers to prioritize a list of features without providing them the opportunity to explore design continuums or dependencies often results in misunderstanding. By facilitating discussions of feature priorities with several customers, you will give them the chance to explore design continuums and relationships that result in a better understanding of market needs.

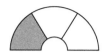

Open-Ended Exploration

Time Frame of Action

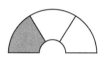

Scalability

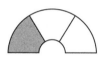

Customer Preparation

Market Preparation

Physical Preparation

Preparing for the Game

You'll need a list of between 8 and 20 features to prioritize, one feature per card. Write the feature on the front of the card and the benefit statements ascribed to this feature on the back because customers will often ask about benefits during the playing of the game (see Figure 2.19). Create three to four identical sets of feature cards because some of the variants of the game described next use more than one set of cards.

FIGURE 2.19 Feature Card

For each feature card that you create, prepare a simple set of design continuums for this feature. A *design continuum* is a set of high-level design alternatives prepared by the development team that helps shape a possible feature. Design continuums usually range from a "low" to a "high," with an associated high-level analysis of the merits and implications of the choice. For example, suppose you were creating a kitchen timer and you were considering the materials for the case. A "low-end" casing could be plastic (cheap, easily colored, easily breakable), a "mid-range" casing could be aluminum (more expensive, durable), and a "high-end" casing could be one of the higher grades of austenitic stainless steel (expensive, durable, resistant to corrosion). This helps prepare you for playing the game; customers will often ask questions about a feature that can be framed around design continuums, with the ensuing discussion providing significant help to the development team in understanding market needs.

Play the game with internal stakeholders (sales, customer service, technical support, the development team) before playing it with real customers. You'll gain valuable insights into the priorities of your team while also increasing your comfort with using this technique. This is especially important when you're unclear of the strategic corporate priorities that are driving your company or your product.

Materials

❑ Feature cards, as described earlier

❑ Additional blank cards to capture new features suggested during the game

Playing the Game

This game is easily explained, and it is best if the facilitator gets started quickly after the explanation is complete. The first two or three features are usually prioritized quickly and easily. The process starts to slow down as customers typically start to ask more questions about new features being added to the growing list and spend more time debating the location of previously prioritized features. Your goal is to encourage the debate, but to do so you'll need to answer their questions about features. Customers often change priorities by adjusting choices on design continuums. For example, customers may start by wanting the "mid-range" aluminum casing, but find themselves accepting the "low-end" plastic casing when more features are added to the prioritization discussion.

The facilitator puts each card on the wall, one card at a time, based on customer feedback.

FIGURE 2.20 Organizing Feature Cards

Customers often want to group features into sets—these three features are A, these are B, and so forth. Do all that you can to avoid this; it makes processing the results more challenging. If you find that you can't guide them against grouping, try making multiple passes over the features. The first pass groups features into must-have, nice-to-have, and don't-care or don't-want features. You should be able to do this fairly quickly. The second pass ranks each of the features contained within these groups.

Customers will sometimes ask you to break a single feature into multiple features, combine two or more features into a single feature, or add a new feature. These are generally good things to do because they will provide you with a greater understanding of customer desires and motivations. The facilitator should be the person who makes this decision.

You can have one facilitator manage the interaction for each group of customers.

FIGURE 2.21 Facilitating Multiple Groups

You may find that "clumps" of customers differ significantly in their prioritization of features, to the point where the facilitator cannot guide the larger team to consensus on the ranking of features. If this happens, and as a matter of last resort, split the single group of customers into two or three smaller groups that can be structured to reach agreement. Do this carefully, however, because the value of this technique is in observing how customers discuss feature priorities and design continuums with each other, and splitting customers by definition limits the debate.

Splitting groups of customers during the game is not the same as forming groups of customers at the beginning of the game and running multiple concurrent discussions. Splitting a group should generally be avoided because the power of the game is watching the group struggle with the prioritizations. Running multiple concurrent discussions, with a single facilitator running each discussion, is a way to compare and contrast the relative prioritizations of different customer groups.

Processing the Results

Processing the results of the *20/20 Vision* game is often quite straightforward. You simply transcribe the final prioritized list, keeping track of significant choices relative to design continuums. The results are then used to inform your product road map, with higher priority features being delivered more quickly.

After you've defined your market-facing priorities, you need to take this list to your development/engineering team and ask them to create a dependency list. You might find that, although your customer ranked a given feature low on their list of features, your technical team has identified it as an essential prerequisite to one or more of the more highly ranked features. As a result, you will find that the final list of features doesn't necessarily match the ranking provided by your customers.

There are other considerations that you should include when preparing the final set of feature priorities. Consider the old adage that goes something like this: "If you try to please everyone, you'll end up pleasing no one." It is true. Keep in mind that each stakeholder affected by the product is likely to have a different ranking of features and that understanding these rankings is critical to producing an effective result. One technique that I find helpful in doing this is to create

Multidimensional Feature Prioritization

20/20 Vision provides essential insights into customer priorities, but it isn't the only information that product managers should use to make feature prioritization choices. Product features can be analyzed according to many different attributes of varying degree of importance. Arguably the most important sets of attributes not captured by this game are the positive and negative economic attributes associated with each feature.

Positive economic attributes include such things as increased revenue, retained customers, brand value, product line synergies, and so forth. Negative attributes include such things as development, distribution, marketing and sales costs, development risk, and opportunity costs. Knowing these is crucial to making sustainable profitable products.

Another important set of attributes is how customer segments react to the presence or absence of features and "how much" of a feature influences their behavior. Kano analysis, which classifies features in four dimensions, can provide further insights into customer desires. The four key dimensions of a Kano analysis are

1. "Surprise and Delight" features. These really make your product stand out from the others. Customers will pay a premium for these features.

2. "More is Better" features. Customers will pay more to get more.

3. "Required" features. You can't sell the product without these features.

4. "Dissatisfiers." Features that customers don't like and avoid about your product. It is unlikely that these features will be present in a *20/20 Vision* game.

Like so many other aspects of product management, feature prioritization is a mixture of science and art. Sorting features according to various attributes certainly helps, but spreadsheets alone won't help you make the right decisions.

a spreadsheet that assigns weightings to features based on stakeholder prioritization and then computes a weighted sum across stakeholders. The advantage of this approach is that it allows you to include an arbitrary number of stakeholders, from customers (by direct customer or by market segment) to service, sales and support, distribution channels, strategic partners, and so forth.

Suppose, for example, that you're ranking features for a blender. You've played the *20/20 Vision* game with four market segments, listed in order of importance: Home Bakers, Parents Who Don't Cook Much, Elementary School Teachers, and Professional Chefs. Your primary market segment is the home market, which by market size is roughly twice as large as the other markets. As a result, you weight the Home Baker so that their votes are the most influential in the process. (See Figure 2.22.)

Putting the results into this kind of spreadsheet can be quite enlightening. In this simple example, we can see that while the Home Baker thinks that the Super Quiet Motor is the third most important potential feature, the other market segments consider it relatively unimportant. The weighted ranking results in this feature being the least important (lower numbers are better in the ranking). As the product manager, you can certainly still put the Super Quiet Motor higher than last place, but you'll be doing this with the knowledge that most of your market considers this to be a relatively unimportant feature. This may be the best choice, based on factors not shown in this small sample (see the sidebar on ranking features). As you can guess, playing around with weightings can produce different results, and the spreadsheet format typically gives you an easy way to explore these options.

A final processing step concerns the handling of negotiations about the relative priority of each feature. It is useful to examine observer cards about which customers negotiated most passionately about the relative ranking of a given feature, as this gives insight into individual customer and customer segment preferences.

| Feature | Rankings | | | | | Weighted Sum | | | | | Final Rank |
	Home Bakers	Parents Who Don't Cook Much	Elementary School Teachers	Professional Chefs	Sums Weightings >>>	Home Bakers	Parents Who Don't Cook Much	Elementary School Teachers	Professional Chefs		
						35	20	15	10		
Automatic-Off Timer	1	2	2	3	135	35	40	30	30		1
Metal Cup	2	4	1	4	205	70	80	15	40		2
Super Quiet Motor	3	5	4	5	315	105	100	60	50		5
Swivel Base	4	3	3	2	265	140	60	45	20		3
Reverse Speed	5	1	5	1	280	175	20	75	10		4

FIGURE 2.22 20/20 Vision Market Feedback

How I Can Use 20/20 Vision

Speed Boat

Identify What Customers Don't Like About Your Product or Service

Customers have complaints. And if you simply ask them to complain, they will. This may be okay, but be careful; the seemingly harmless snowflakes of a few minor problems can quickly become an avalanche of grievances from which you can never recover. I've sat through a few of these "let it all hang out and complain about anything sessions," and just about everyone leaves the room tired and frustrated. Think "angry mob" and make certain you know where the exits are located.

It doesn't have to be this way. You can ask your customers what's bothering them if you do it in a way that lets you stay in control of how complaints are stated and discussed. In the process, you'll find fresh new ideas for the changes you can make to address your customers' most important concerns.

The Game

Draw a boat on a whiteboard or sheet of butcher paper. You'd like the boat to really move fast. Unfortunately, the boat has a few anchors holding it back. The boat is your system, and the features that your customers don't like are its anchors.

Customers write what they don't like on an index card and place it under the boat as an anchor. They can also estimate how much faster the boat would go if that anchor were cut and add that to the card. Estimates of speed are really estimates of pain. Customers can also annotate the anchors created by other customers, indicating agreement on substantial topics. When customers are finished posting their anchors, review each one, carefully confirming your understanding of what they want to see changed in the system.

Why It Works

Although most customers have complaints, few customers are genuinely "against" you or your product. Even if they express extreme frustration, the reality is that they want to succeed when using your product (see the sidebar "*Speed Boat* for Expensive Products"). Giving them a way to express their frustration *without* letting a group mentality or a single person dominate the discussion is what most customers want. *Speed Boat* creates this relatively safe environment where customers can tell you what's wrong.

Another significant reason that *Speed Boat* works is that many people don't feel comfortable expressing their frustrations verbally. Giving them a chance to write things down gives them a way to provide feedback. It also gives them an opportunity to reflect on what is genuinely most important. The opportunity to reflect is especially important for those customers who just seem to be somewhat unhappy people (you know, the ones who complain a lot about the little details). Asking them to verbalize their issues, especially in writing, motivates them to *think* about these issues. Many of them will identify trivial issues as just that—trivial issues—and, in the process, focus on the truly big issues. Thus, they end up voicing their complaints, but they're put into perspective. When they get used to *thinking* about their complaints, especially quantifying what the impact is, they are more reasonable and will contribute more to success—theirs and yours.

However, there are products for which the sheer number of seemingly trivial complaints

Open-Ended Exploration

Time Frame of Action

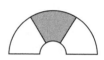

Scalability

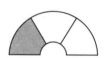

Customer Preparation

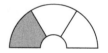

Market Preparation

Physical Preparation

adds up to one truly large complaint—the product or service offering might have been good enough to purchase, but not good enough to continue using or to recommend to others. In this case, *Speed Boat* helps you identify the set of problems that you need to address before your product fails. Although we don't require that customers use different sized or shaped anchors, the game does not prevent customers from changing the size, shape, weight, or number of anchors that they add to the boat.

PREPARING FOR THE GAME

Use the best possible imagery that you can to keep the mood playful. Buy pictures of boats and stickers of fish at stores that stock school or craft supplies and post them on a whiteboard. Print anchors on your index cards. Keeping the mood playful helps everyone deal with the potentially stressful content of the feedback. Aladdin Knowledge Systems, Inc., the world's leading provider of hardware-based software antipiracy solutions, went so far as to merge a fast boat with a USB dongle to create vivid imagery that helped set the proper tone for their session (see Figure 2.23). You can also go "lo tech" for your boat, which the Greater Boston Chapter of the ACM did when they played *Speed Boat*. In this game, Tobias Mayer simply drew a speed boat on a chalk board (see Figure 2.24).

Steve Peacock of Air Transport IT described a variant of this game he played with customers at an annual users conference. Instead of using anchors, they referred to complaints as barnacles. Barnacles were of three sizes—small, medium, and large—where the size represented the strength of the complaint.

Although you want customers who can, and will, contribute, avoid including any customers who are likely to be overly dominant or negative. If you must invite such customers, consider running two *Speed Boat* sessions: one for the unruly crowd and another for the quieter, more thoughtful crowd.

FIGURE 2.23 Aladdin Knowledge System's Speed Boat Design

It helps to review your service and support systems to identify any specific items that may exist for customers coming to the event, because they use this opportunity to ask pointed questions about the status of reported problems. It also helps to make certain you're aware of any plans to address known problems. Although it is important to try to avoid addressing issues during the game, there are times that you will have to do this, so be prepared.

Materials

❑ Pictures of a speed boat

❑ Anchor cards

❑ 5"×8" cards that customers can use as simulated anchors to capture their concerns

FIGURE 2.24 ACM's Simple Speed Boat Design

Playing the Game

After the facilitator introduces the game, give customers a few minutes to gather their thoughts before you expect them to create anchors. Then, to help get the process of posting the anchors to the wall started, the facilitator should gently ask a few customers for completed anchor cards and tape these to the wall on behalf of the customer. After this is done, other customers will spontaneously join in and add anchors. There is no requirement that customers take turns posting anchors. In fact, the game works better if several customers and the facilitator are posting anchors at the same time because there is a formal review process.

Participants walk up to the wall, add their anchors, and return to their seats.

FIGURE 2.25 Posting Anchor Cards

No Defensive Response—Even if They Are Wrong!

One of the hardest things about *Speed Boat* is not responding to customers during the game—especially when they write an anchor that is just wrong! This is where good facilitation skills are critical. In these situations the facilitator must keep the focus on understanding the issue presented by the customer. There will be plenty of time to address the customer after the event. And chances are you'll want to communicate this to all of your customers because chances are good that more than one will share this misunderstanding.

When customers have finished posting anchors, the facilitator begins the review process (see Figure 2.26). Try to review *every single anchor*. This lets your customers know that their feedback is important. The approach that works best is to let customers finish adding anchors, and then ask them to be seated. Walk up to the anchors and review each one. Although only one customer created the anchor, invite the whole group to comment on what was written. As you review the anchor, it is *critically important* that you refrain from trying to solve the problem, respond to the feedback, or justify why a certain choice is made. Doing this will dramatically change the game dynamic. Instead of encouraging forthright and sincere discussions of perceived problems, customers will interpret your response as a defense mechanism and will quickly become guarded in their communication and cynical of the process. Seek to understand the underlying reason why this anchor is holding them back from success, not in responding to or justifying the status quo.

Facilitator reviews each card with the customers. Observers keep track of what was said.

FIGURE 2.26 Reviewing the Anchor Cards

There are practical reasons why you should not attempt to address or respond to anchors during the game. You probably don't have all the data needed to make a thorough response. You probably don't have all the necessary decision makers in the same room. You are almost certainly violating your product development and product management practices by making decisions in this manner. Perhaps most seriously, you're probably not in the right frame of mind to address these concerns, and you don't want to let the stress you may feel during this game result in short-sighted decisions.

Note that reviewing every single anchor doesn't necessarily mean reading or sharing each anchor. Sometimes it is better to quickly group anchors with similar content and/or themes and talk about these anchors as a group. This means that you need to continually scan the anchors that are being added during the game to see if there are obvious trends. In rare cases, you can move anchors that customers have added to start the process of group formation during the exercise.

The spatial arrangement of the anchors usually has important meanings to the participants. One example has already been mentioned—grouping similar cards. Sometimes customers will naturally put "heavier" or "larger" anchors near the bottom, or designate that there is more than one boat, where different boats have different meanings. To preserve the spatial memory of the exercise, take many photos during the game. Always take photos of the final card arrangement.

Consider asking customers to vote on the top three or five anchors whose removal would have the most positive impact on the boat's speed.

One variant that can be useful is to ask customers to add "engines" to the boats after they've finished. The engines represent features that can "overpower" the anchors and enable the boat to move faster. Do this carefully, because it changes the focus and dynamics of the game. If you really think that you need to focus on adding features, consider *Product Box*, *Buy a Feature*, or *Prune the Product Tree*. Sometimes, however, the energy of the room changes and the participants naturally start talking about adding features. When this happens, go with the flow and add some horsepower to your boats.

Processing the Results

The goal of processing this feedback is to classify each anchor (or common grouping of anchors) according to three key attributes:

- The specific area of the product associated with the problem
- The severity of the problem
- The priority or urgency of fixing it

Begin this process by transcribing the anchors into a spreadsheet or other system that you use to track product requirements. When there is more than one anchor around a common complaint, record the number of anchors that related to this complaint. Determine the root cause or area of the product associated with the problem. Here are some common root causes:

- Poor documentation—Incorrect, improper, misleading, outdated, incomprehensible, and so on.
- User inexperience—Users didn't know that something could be done with your product.
- Defect—An error or bug in your product. It is best if you explore this just enough to confirm that you understand the problem, so that you can correlate it with your defect-tracking system.
- Technology incompatibility—A previously unknown or improperly communicated incompatibility with your product.
- Mismatched expectations—For example, a customer expected the fountain pen to work while on a plane and expressed frustration when it didn't.

As you're processing the cards, be certain to include photos of the original cards written by your customers, because there is both meaning in the spatial arrangement of the cards and a certain empathy and intimacy that comes from working directly with your customers' feedback. In some cases you can even get a sense for the passion a customer has about a given topic by looking at the card they've created. I've seen cards with lightening bolts, frowns, "!#@&!#", phrases like "grrrr," or statements punctuated with several exclamation points. All of these are reflective of a customer who cares pretty deeply about the topic. Retaining this information is important to motivating your team to action.

Characterize the perceived severity of the problem. A common approach used in managing bugs associated with software systems is to assign each bug a numeric ranking from 1 to 5.[9] Even if you're not working on a software system, you might find that this list provides you with a useful way of characterizing customer feedback.

1. Crash with no workaround. Often associated with unavoidable data loss, and typically considered the worst kind of bug. For nonsoftware-based products, this kind of problem could be considered equivalent to a serious safety issue that motivates a product recall. Using this as a baseline, you can adjust the rest of the rankings in a way that makes sense for your product.

2. Crash with workaround.

3. Serious problem.

4. Minor problem.

5. Not a bug (something the customer reported as a problem, but isn't).

Characterize the priority of fixing the problem, again using a numerical ranking from 1 to 5:

1. Immediate—The problem must be fixed immediately, with the updated product delivered to customers as quickly as possible.

2. Urgent—The problem must be fixed before the next major product milestone.

3. Before next release—The problem must be fixed before the next version of the product is released to customers.

4. As time allows—Although it would be nice to fix this problem before the next release, customers can live with the problem.

5. Defer—We understand that at least one customer perceives this as a problem, but we're going to explicitly defer addressing the issue.

It is relatively easy to create consistency within your organization for severities, because they can be objectively verified. Priorities, on the other hand, are subjective. A misspelling in your documentation may get a "4" for severity, but different cultures will ascribe different priorities to fixing such a problem. I've found that Americans and Europeans are more tolerant and are happy to give these kinds of problems correspondingly low priorities. Japanese customers tend not to be as tolerant and give documentation bugs high priorities. Because of the subjective nature of bug priorities, use a cross-functional team approach to establish priorities. As you can guess, high severity problems correlate with high-priority fixes.

Even this level of analysis may be insufficient when making a good choice on how to handle a problem. Consider that sometimes trying to fix a Severity One problem (crash with no work-around) could cause other problems. This situation often happens in older software systems, and makes deciding what to fix extremely challenging.

Review the final results, organized by priority, to define how you will address each priority. It is especially important to communicate your choices to your customers so that they can understand how you're addressing their feedback.

9. You should adapt this list to the ranking system used by your company.

How I Can Use Speed Boat

Part Three
TOOLS AND TEMPLATES

Part One of this book provided you with a foundation for understanding and applying Innovation Games. Part Two examined each game in detail, showing you how to prepare for, play, and then post-process the results of each game. Part Three compliments Part One and Part Two by providing you with tools and templates that you can use to begin playing Innovation Games with your customers. It provides an expanded overview of planning and includes sample letters that you can use to invite customers to the game and thank them when it's over. It ends with FAQs and some expanded advice on facilitating a great game.

Phase One Planning in Greater Detail

Although the core of phase one event planning is answering the "Five Ws" listed in Part One, our experience is that successfully planning an Innovation Game requires you to consider a fairly comprehensive set of questions. This section provides additional questions for your consideration, organized around the core questions presented in Part One. If you're going to do a lot of planning, you might consider using the resources available from the Meeting Professionals International web site, www.mpiweb.org.

Whom are you inviting? Consider customers and your internal project team both.

- Whom are you going to invite (customers)? Whereas the discussion of segmentation strategies in Part One provides broad guidance on whom to invite, in this phase you'll have to identify specific people. A common question is, "What if the people we want to invite compete against each other?" Our experience is that unless your product is fundamentally tied to the axis of competition, chances are good that direct competitors will participate in the game and you'll get good results. This happened to us when working with a Fortune 100 client on a product launch exercise. The client selected *Product Box* and had invited several large customers and partners to participate. This was not a problem, because our client's product was not the axis of competition among these customers.

A related question concerns the power structure of the participants. We've run sessions where managers grabbed control of the game, completely ignoring the input of their subordinates. In other sessions, managers and subordinates collaborated to produce extraordinary results. There are no firm rules, but try to remain aware of the relationships that exist between game participants.

- Whom are you going to invite (internal project team)? As outlined in Part One, a cross-functional project team that enables you to staff for all the roles in a team is the best structure. In terms of cross-functional teams, consider asking representatives from all areas of your company, including marketing, sales, service, development, executives, quality assurance, and technical publications.

- How many customers will you invite? A good rule is between 12 and 36, because research has shown that 12 customers are expected to represent 70% to 75% of market needs, and 30 customers can be expected to represent 90% of market needs.

- Will you coordinate and/or pay for their travel? As the host, you need to determine the degree to which you will be planning and/or paying for your customers' travel. You need to tell customers as early as you can about this so that they can prepare accordingly. If you're conducting the event at a hotel, you should get a significant discount on rooms.

What will you be doing? Consider both the games and related event activities.

- What do you need them to do to prepare for the event? Be as detailed as possible; few things frustrate a customer more than not having the opportunity to prepare for a game.

- What else, in addition to the games, are you planning to do at the event? Are you planning on "fun" activities? What do your customers need to bring to fully enjoy these activities?

- Will you be doing something before the event? Customers' travel plans can vary by quite a bit, and although some customers might be able to drive to the event, others may be traveling quite a long distance. In these circumstances I recommend having an optional dinner or reception the night before the event.

Why are you doing these things? **Why** should your customer come? Consider your customer understanding and customer relationship goals.

- Why are you asking customers to come? What is the benefit to them? You need to give your customers a reason to come—literally. What's in it for them? The good news is that if you've followed the market research process, answering this question should be fairly easy.

Mentioning Innovation Games in the Invitation

Customers should be given an overview of what they'll be doing at the event, including what they need to do to prepare for the game, but it isn't a requirement to explicitly state that they'll be playing an Innovation Game. For example, when Aladdin Knowledge Systems invited customers to participate in their Security Council meeting, they never mentioned that customers would be playing *Speed Boat* or *Buy a Feature*. Instead, the agenda items for these games were described as "An opportunity to share current pain points with Aladdin representatives and to provide insight and direction to potential future HASP product features."

Of course, explicitly mentioning that customers are playing an Innovation Game can pique curiosity and generate excitement. When Emerson Climate Technologies chose to use *Spider Web* at their 2006 Technology Advisory Council meeting, they described it as follows:

> **Give us your vision**
> Help fuel innovation by letting Emerson know what you really value in future versions of our products and services. Instead of reviewing developed products, you will develop the requirements for the products and software that will eventually serve your and the industry's needs. The Enthiosys Innovation Games are proven techniques to create innovative products and services.

You should feel free to choose the approach that you feel most comfortable with.

- Will you compensate them? Although rare, there are some situations, such as when you're going to take your customers away from an important job, or when participating in the games might cause them financial hardship, where you might consider compensating them for their participation in your game.
- You may also consider whether you will be giving attendees a small token of your appreciation for attending the event. You can be as creative as you wish because there is an entire industry of promotional products at your disposal.

When is the event?

- How long is the event? A good rule is two hours per game, with no more than three games in one day.
- Have you remembered to include refreshment and bathroom breaks? Have you allocated buffer time in your schedule?

Where is the event?

- Have you provided full logistics information and directions?
- Does this location provide the necessary infrastructure (A/V, Internet, electrical, wall space, room space) for your event?

You may need to consider a few additional questions:

- If you're a public company and you're going to discuss potential future product plans, you may need to prepare and recite a "safe harbor" statement from your legal team before the game.

- Similarly, if you're a public company and there is a chance that pricing or price-related issues may be discussed, you may also need to recite an anti-trust and/or similar statement from your legal team.
- Do you need them to sign an NDA?
- Do you need them to assign all rights to the ideas discussed to your company as a condition for participation in the game?

Customizing Games for Your Event

One of the more common questions concerns the degree to which Innovation Games can be tailored to meet specific situations. Although you should feel comfortable in modifying these games to meet your needs, avoid doing so until you've gained experience in the techniques as they are presented. If you do tailor the games, it is best to do so in the context of long-established and strong customer relationships.

An example of a company that has successfully tailored Innovation Games is AirIT, a leading provider of turnkey, integrated software solutions to the transportation industry. AirIT's flagship product is PROPworks, a comprehensive software program designed to manage the lease, property, and revenue information needed to operate complicated businesses and transportation facilities of all sizes. This includes airports, seaports, and railroads, as well as large national and global commercial enterprises.

AirIT has become fairly sophisticated in their use of Innovation Games, trying them in several novel formats and extending the basic concept by trying out new kinds of games at their annual user's conference. In this section I'll describe three variations of the games that AirIT created for their 2005 user's conference. I'm doing this so that you can see how others have tailored the games for their unique situation.

The common theme in all of AirIT's choices was not using a facilitator. Instead, AirIT created a very relaxed way to play the games over the two-day user's conference through the use of a "Think Tank." In their design, the "Think Tank" was an open room where you could play the games and share ideas with AirIT employees.

Overall, AirIT was pleased with their results (as you can see in their client-facing thank you letter later in Part Three). One area of common disappointment with this approach for all three games was that because they didn't use a facilitator, they were not able to deeply explore their customers' intentions or desires relative to the various games they played. Future events will probably focus on more traditional facilitation.

Customizing *Speed Boat*

AirIT made two modifications to this game. First, they renamed it after their product, calling it *PROPworks—Ship of State* game. Second, they made the following changes to the game play:

- Instead of a speed boat, they used a picture of a large ship.

- Instead of anchors, they invited customers to write their comments on "barnacles" that were attached to the ship, making it slower.

- They didn't play the game with a facilitator. Instead, they opened up the game and allowed customers to add barnacles anytime over the two-day user conference.

Customizing *Product Box*

AirIT made three modifications to the game. First, like *Speed Boat*, they renamed it to match their product line, calling it the *PROP-box Game*. Second, they adopted the variant of the game in which they awarded a prize for the best box. They modified the game play as follows:

- Instead of having all customers design their boxes at the same time, they provided materials in specially designed rooms and encouraged customers to design their boxes between the end of lunch on the first day and the beginning of lunch on the second day of the conference.

- All boxes were placed on a "store shelf" in a common area. During the afternoon refreshment break of the second day, four "secret shoppers" looked over the boxes and voted for a winner. The winner was the box with the most votes.

Customizing *Buy a Feature*

In this case, AirIT leveraged the location of the event, Washington, D.C., to help customize the game. Instead of offering features for sale, they offered features for purchase through contributions to a "Political Action Committee." As recommended by the game, they offered money to each attendee of the conference and priced features in a way that forced customers to work together (no one customer could purchase a feature). Feature purchases were tracked in an openly visible way so that when one feature was purchased,

other members of the PROPpac (PropWorks Political Action Committee) would not have to further consider it. This game probably suffered the most from the lack of a facilitator because the rich negotiations between customers about who wanted what feature were lost. Even still, the event provided a rich opportunity for AirIT to gain a better understanding of customer desires.

Sample Agenda for an Innovation Game

Pam Oliver is the product manager for Blendz, a fictitious manufacturer of commercial food and drink blenders. Here is a sample document that captures the work Pam and her internal team put together for a one-day Customer Advisory Council meeting. The templates are invaluable for making certain that key decisions are written down and that everyone on your internal team understands their role in the process. You can customize this sample agenda to fit your needs:

Purpose

The purpose of this document is to record the agenda for the March 13 Blendz Customer Advisory Council meeting and capture key decisions regarding this event.

Background and Logistics

The spring session of the twice-yearly meeting of the Blendz Customer Advisory Council will be held March 13 in Detroit, MI. As of January 9, 18 customers have confirmed. We expect no more than 24 customers. Although Blendz corporate headquarters is located in Topeka, KS, a large number of our customers are located within a single plane flight of Detroit, MI.

Key Goals

The key goals for this Customer Advisory Council Meeting are as follows:

- Provide an opportunity for Blendz customers to share how they use various Blendz product features.
- Provide Blendz with opportunities for product and service innovation by uncovering unmet market needs.
- Provide Blendz with information that will inform near- and long-term product development road maps.
- Foster a creative sense of shared development and discovery.

To accomplish these goals, Blendz has elected to play the *Product Box* and the *Buy a Feature* Innovation Games with members of the Blendz Customer Advisory Council. We will start with the *Product Box* game so that participants are more likely to express their own ideas about what is important about their Blendz blender, because they will not yet have seen our ideas about potential new features. To provide extra motivation, we will allow council members to vote on the best overall product box. The winner will receive a $50 coupon.

Following this, we will play the *Buy a Feature* game. Pam Oliver prepared a sample list of features and their suggested prices and proposed the amount of money that will be given to each participant (see "Key Remaining Action Items"). Some participants will receive more money than others based on their perceived importance to the company. If more than one participant is present from the same company, the amount of money will be distributed equally among company participants, and they will be put into the same group. Because we expect to have three groups of customers engaged in each exercise, we require one *Buy a Feature* leader for each group. Pam Oliver, Stephan Zunck, and Robert Derby (see Table 3.1) will manage the selling of features for each product group.

Table 3.1 Blendz Team

Role	Description
Planner	Pam Oliver, Product Manager
Organizer	Franklin Smith, Assistant to the VP of the Fast-Food Sales Division
Greeter	Pam Oliver
Facilitator	Raj Subramanian, Director of Customer Service
	Group leaders for *Buy a Feature:* • Pam Oliver • Stephan Zunck, Product Manager • Robert Derby, Marketing Director
Helper	Franklin Smith
Observer(s)	Timothy Melna, Design and Packaging Services
	Sarah Johnston, Materials Engineer
	Dan Allstead, Retail Channel Manager
	Randy Weaver, VP, Sales
Photographer	Clifford Mark, eCommerce website developer

Key Remaining Action Items

The following action items must be handled before the event:

1. (Owner: Franklin) Finalize event location, sign contracts, and prepare for the event.

2. (Owner: Pam) Finalize list of features, feature prices, and amount of money given to participants.

3. (Owner: Franklin) Acquire materials for the *Product Box* game.

Room Layout and Customer Organization

We need to carefully plan for this meeting because it will contain a large number of people. We will need a room that can support round tables (no more than eight people per table) or square tables that can be configured as shown in Figure 3.1. The room will need to have additional tables for Blendz employees. We will need one additional table for storing supplies and for the product box gallery.

Customers will be organized into three tables with at least six and no more than eight customers per table. Figure 3.1 shows a representative room layout for a *Product Box* exercise conducted with two groups of customers, with six to eight customers in each group. Note that

- Tables are covered in easel paper to encourage doodling/creativity.
- Product boxes and props are placed in the front of the room to foster a sense of discovery and creativity.
- Tables are organized so that participants work in rather close proximity, facing each other.
- There is a small stand in the front of the room to hold a projector should one be needed.
- The room must be big enough to support 40 to 60 people.[1]

FIGURE 3.1 Setting Up the Room

---

1. Keep in mind that you need a room roughly twice as large as the number of total participants, customers, and members of your team. You want to create a relaxed environment, with enough room to rearrange tables if needed during the course of the event.

Detailed Schedule

March 12— Afternoon

Blendz Customer Advisor Council arrives. Dinner event at the hotel hosted by Pam.

Hotel must grant unfettered access to the meeting room starting at 6 p.m. to allow for setup.

March 13

7:30AM	All	Participants invited to room for continental breakfast, coffee.
		Participants are guided to appropriate seating locations.
8:00AM	Pam	Welcome and brief opening remarks.
8:15AM	Raj	*Product Box* exercise described.
8:30AM	Raj	*Product Box* exercise initiated.

> **Note:** It helps to play upbeat music while people create their product boxes, as such music contributes to the overall "fun" atmosphere you're trying to create.

9:30AM		Break

> **Note:** You want to schedule a few breaks and offer them to customers. Don't force them to take a break, however. If your customers want to continue creating their product boxes, let them. To help signify a break, consider changing the music or playing it more loudly.

9:45AM	Raj	Product box sales presentations. Raj will select the initial presenter from a hat; each presenter will pick the next presenter from the hat until all have had a chance to sell their box.
10:45AM		Buffer

> **Note:** Your agendas should always have plenty of buffer time!

11:00AM	Franklin	Carefully gather product boxes and put them in the back of the room to create a product box gallery.
11:30AM		Working Lunch

> **Note:** When you're playing a game you should always plan on using the lunch session to clean up the results of the previous game and prepare for the next. 60 minutes is usually good for a light working lunch, 90 minutes for a more elaborate lunch.

12:30PM		Product box voting and Award Ceremony.
1:00PM	Raj	*Buy a Feature* exercise described.
1:15PM	Team	*Buy a Feature* engaged.
2:15PM		Buffer
2:30PM		Break
3:00PM	Pam	Closing remarks, gathering initial feedback from customers.
5:00PM		Session ends
6:30PM		Shared event for those who are staying the night.

March 14

7:30AM	Team	Breakfast/review meeting of product boxes and key insights gained from the previous day. We will do this by posting notes generated by observers along with key slogans from product boxes on a wall, looking for similarities and patterns. We will also review the specific features purchased by each customer team.
11:00AM	Team	Break for airport. Flights after 12:00 noon are okay.

Sample Invitation Letter

As detailed in Part One, the invitation letter you send to your customers needs to answer the questions you can expect participants will ask. Examples include

- Basic event logistics: Where? When? How long? Typically half to a full day.
- Will you pay for their travel?
- Will you coordinate their travel?
- What is the overall agenda?
- Who will be coming?
- What do they need to do to prepare?

To illustrate, page 138 shows a copy of the letter I sent to executives of Rally Software Development for our 2005 Enthiosys Customer Appreciation Day. Although some of the letter is clearly boiler plate, you can also see that I try to customize the letter.

Thank You Letter Template

Page 139 shows a template that you can use as the foundation for your follow-up thank you letter. You will have to tailor the letter in the following ways:

- Change the name of the group to match the name of your customer meeting. The sample letter assumes that you've played the games in the context of your Customer Advisory Board.
- Change the reference to the meeting frequency. The sample letter assumes a quarterly meeting of the Customer Advisory Board.

AirIT Sample Thank You Letter

Reprinted with their permission, pages 140 and 141 show a copy of the letter AirIT sent to attendees of their 2005 PropWorks user conference. Note that this letter contains several design elements of a well-written thank you letter:

- It starts by thanking customers for attending.
- It clearly restates the motivation for the conference and the genuine desire for customer participation.
- It portrays, in a warm and humanizing manner, the reason for trying Innovation Games.
- It outlines the results of playing the games, and at times outlines some of the specific issues taken to address user-identified issues.
- It lets customers know that the artwork they have created provides enduring value to the organization.

It is an excellent model for you to use in your own letters.

Dear Ryan, Tim, and Dean

I am honored to serve Rally as a member of the Rally Technical Advisory Board and to count Rally as a client of Enthiosys. In the short time that we've been working together, I've gained a great appreciation of how seriously you take building for the future needs of your many diverse customers, and I am especially excited about facilitating the *Prune the Product Tree* game at your Customer Summit in a few weeks.

Enthiosys has grown to the point where it is now our turn to take a step back and share an event that we hope will help us better understand how we can effectively meet your needs through future product and service offerings. By attending this event, you will have the chance to work directly with Enthiosys employees and other Enthiosys customers in directly shaping the future of Enthiosys products and services. We will also be taking this opportunity to provide feedback on our activities over the past year and to provide you with an overview of our future plans. More plainly, we're practicing what we preach.

The event will take place in Monterey, CA, at the Monterey Plaza Hotel and Spa (http://www.woodsidehotels.com/monterey/monte_home.htm). We have negotiated special rates with the hotel for this weekend, so please let them know that you're associated with this event. (You are responsible for travel and hotel room costs. Enthiosys will pay for food.) Dress code is business casual, and we recommend that you bring something warm because Monterey can be a bit cooler than you might expect.

Our schedule is as follows:

Thursday, Sept. 22 (travel day):
6:30 p.m.   Casual dinner reception at The Whaling Station, a short walk from the hotel.

Friday, Sept. 23
9:00 a.m.   Check in
10:00 a.m.   Welcome
11:00 a.m.   Keynote—Don Nielson, SRI
12:00 p.m.   Lunch
1:00 p.m.   Innovation Games sessions
3:00 p.m.   Wrap Up

Saturday, Sept. 24 and Sunday, Sept. 25

Although we have nothing formally planned, you may want to extend your stay over the weekend to enjoy the many attractions and activities in Monterey.

We are pleased to announce Don Nielson as our guest speaker. Don is a recently retired vice president of the SRI who has just published *A Heritage of Innovation: SRI's First Half Century*, which chronicles the many innovations of SRI in its first 50 years. You can learn more about Don's work at http://www.sri.com/about/history/nielson_book.html. We will distribute copies of his book at the event along with a few extra "goodies" that we're sure you'll enjoy.

We respectfully request that you RSVP by email or phone no later than September 12 so that we can provide the hotel with an accurate head count for planning purposes.

On behalf of the Enthiosys team, I am again honored to send you this invitation and look forward to seeing you at this event.

Regards,
Luke Hohmann
CEO
Enthiosys, Inc.
Innovation Through Understanding
cell: (408) 529-0319
www.enthiosys.com

Sample Invitation Letter

Dear <Customer Advisory Board Participant>

On behalf of the entire <company> team, I want to thank you for joining us at our quarterly Customer Advisor Board meeting. Your candid feedback on how we can improve our products and services is warmly appreciated. The purpose of this letter is to give you some insight into our key learnings from this and other customer-facing activities and how we have taken steps to act on your feedback.

We believe that the three most important <areas for improvement or topics to address in future releases of our product> you told us were

1. You require additional training and reference materials.

2. You would like to be able to customize the location of the flange and mounting bolts to provide for greater flexibility when installing custom motors.

3. <topic or area for improvement #3>

In addition to these specific areas of improvement, this Customer Advisory Board meeting provided similar feedback to our last Customer Advisory Board meeting in December 2005, in which you requested more "best practices" training and additional technical information.

We are working to respond to this feedback and have instituted the following changes.

1. We have modified our website to include a far greater emphasis on "best practice" training. You can access this information at www.companyname.com\training.

2. We are currently working with our manufacturing team to determine how we could provide more flexible options for the location of the flange and mounting bolts. We intend to report on our progress at the next Customer Advisory Board meeting.

You will continue to receive letters from us as we work to address your feedback and make improvements to our products and services. Thank you again for your participation in the Customer Advisory Board. If you have any further questions or suggestions, please feel free to contact myself or <contact person>.

Regards,
Dignitary
Title

Thank You Letter Template

Air-Transport IT Services, Inc.
6675 Westwood Blvd., Suite 210
Orlando, FL 32821
Phone: 407-370-4664
Fax: 407-370-4657

June 30, 2005

Dear PROPworks® Users:

I missed seeing everyone at the User Conference this year, but I would like to take this opportunity to thank the attendees for taking the time to come, and furthermore for participating in the "Think Tank Games." Since so many of you eagerly participated in the games, I thought it would be nice to address you with this letter (sent with the PROPworks® Newsletter) to let you know a little bit about the background and results of the games.

As you know over the past three or four years at the User Conference, we've looked for ways to get feedback on PROPworks®. It was in Fort Lauderdale in 2003 that I announced that if any three or more PROPworks® sites could agree on an enhancement request for a report, that we would include it in the next released version. Last year in Los Angeles we announced and posted a survey on the AirIT Support survey web site. The participation in these feedback events was low, and thus we searched for a new way for you to tell us about PROPworks®.

We had already determined that some kind of survey would be conducted at the User Conference. In April of this year, shortly after the agenda for the User Conference was finalized, I attended a software development conference, and was exposed to the exercises that became the "Think Tank Games." If you want more information about the games, and where they came from, you can find it at www.enthiosys.com. Knowing that the only unscheduled component of the User Conference was the Campground, or Think Tank as it was called this year, I talked to Geoff and Angela about including the games as a method of gathering feedback. While the games are designed to be played in a meeting session with a facilitator, we adapted the three games: PROPpac, PROPworks® Ship of State, and PROPbox so that they could be played in the rather open and unstructured environment of the Think Tank. For the most part reaction to the games has been very positive, of those responding to the User Conference survey there was only one negative response.

Each game is targeted to get some specific feedback on PROPworks®. Through the PROPworks® Ship of State game, we hoped to find out what you thought was "not right" about PROPworks®. With the PROPpac game, we wanted to find out how, with limited resources, you would seek to improve PROPworks®. Finally, by playing the PROPbox game, we wanted you to tell us what things you think provide the value of PROPworks®

Dealing with the negative first, let's take a look at the PROPworks® Ship of State game. This game went a little awry as we had intended to have three "sizes" (small, medium, large) of barnacles present, and the size of the barnacle would indicate the level of pain the problem caused. When I first started looking at the poster and results it was scary because it appeared that a fourth size of barnacle, extra large, had been added and almost all the barnacles were extra large. I later found out that the original barnacles could not be found at the beginning of the conference, and initially only the extra large size was available. Overall, 26 barnacles were attached to the ship. Close to one-forth (six of the barnacles) were related to opinions on the User Conference and product support or were completely unreadable. Of the remaining 20 items, there were a number that were related to configuration issues and about six or seven items were "new" issues to AirIT staff that had not been previously raised. Last month TechNote dealt with the password configuration issues, which was identified in about six barnacles, and Pat Williamson has taken on the task of writing up a white paper to deal with the other issues raised in this game in detail.

The PROPpac game may have been my favorite. In some ways it is a way of allowing you to experience what the PROPworks® CCB (Configuration Control Board) does on a monthly basis. Here are a number of great

 Fraport   *AirIT is a wholly-owned subsidiary of Fraport – Frankfurt Airport Services Worldwide*

AirIT Sample Thank You Letter

ideas, but they each have a cost, and the resources are limited. How do you determine which ones to implement? As it meets each month the CCB either assigns the request to a version, identifies it as a good idea, but puts it off in a generic "future" version, or rejects the request. In some cases, the CCB would like more feedback before taking action. So this year eighteen of the items that the CCB sought more feedback on were placed into the PROPpac game. Each user organization (airport/port) was given 3600 PROPbucks to spend. Of the 18 items on the list, seven were sold and will be targeted for PROPworks® 7.0. Interestingly enough, 68,400 PROPbucks were distributed, but only 61,000 were collected. That means that 7400 PROPbucks were outstanding, and there were seven unsold items on the list that had a price of under 7400. It is curious to me as to why you left that many PROPbucks on the table and if anyone would like to provide some feedback, either email me or use the PROPworks® Support Forum. Some of the AirIT staff have said that some of you wanted to keep your PROPbucks because they were "cute," and maybe that was why they didn't all get spent. I don't know about cute, but if anyone wants an uncut sheet of PROPmeet 2005 PROPbucks, just drop me an email and I'll see you get it.

The PROPbox game was apparently a hit for everyone that participated, and it probably didn't hurt that a PROPY was on the line. Trying to come up with some way to analyze the results has been a challenge. There were 133 textual items (phrases or words) that were placed on the six boxes that were created. Of these items, about 40% of them were listing the features of the product, and over half of these items were about the Agreement and Billing modules. In addition, things that were important to those of you doing the boxes also include the versatility of PROPworks® , the user interface, and the Support and Maintenance that AirIT offers. Also, more than one box touted the "feature" of the annual PROPworks® User Conference. The boxes that made it back to Orlando are displayed on a shelf in the computer room, and provide a great deal of satisfaction for all the members of the AirIT team, even those that you don't see at the User Conference, as they serve as a confirmation that no matter how many barnacles we may encounter, PROPworks® provides you with a positive experience. We sincerely thank you for all the kind things you put on the boxes.

Looking back on the game experience, it would appear that there are several things that can be done to improve the games if they are played at a future conference. At least one game "discussion" session needs to be included. The question is whether each game should have a session, or should there be a single session to cover all the games. Some have suggested that having three games was at least one too many and that folks' attention was too diluted as a result. From my point of view overseeing first ABT and now PROPworks® development for the past eleven years, these games have provided more feedback than anything that we've tried in the past and I would like to see them continue in some form at future User Conferences. Let us here at AirIT know your thoughts on whether the games should return and what you would do to improve them.

Sincerely,

Steven Peacock
Senior Vice-President Development

Table 3.2 Basic Materials

Item	Purpose
❏ Pens and pencils	Allows customers to take notes
❏ Note pads (one per person)	Allows customer to take notes
❏ Easels (min two)	Allows you to capture shared notes for the group
❏ Post-It Easel Paper	Excellent choice because you can stick it to most walls without tape and without harming the wall. Easel paper is also a good substitute for plain butcher paper when you need to cover a wall or a table quickly. When hanging easel paper, do it as shown in Figure 3.2.

Basic Materials Checklists

Room

Bigger rooms are better. In general, ask for a room that is 50 percent bigger than the number of total participants (customers and members of your team). Room setup can take anywhere from three to six hours, so it is best to have access to the room the night before the event.

Basic Materials for All Games

Table 3.2 shows the basic materials that you will need for all games described in this book. Game-specific materials are described with each game and described further here.

These items are typically provided by the hotel or place that is hosting the event (such as a meeting or conference center). If you're holding the event at your company, you'll need to provide them.

You need to supply the items from Table 3.3.

Product Box Materials (per table)

- ❏ Two or three product box props (for example, old cereal boxes)
- ❏ One blank bright-white product box for each participant

- ❏ Sharp-tip felt markers
- ❏ Large gold "star" stickers
- ❏ Three pairs of scissors
- ❏ Three rolls of Scotch tape
- ❏ Colored markers
- ❏ Yarn in assorted colors—red/blue/green
- ❏ Stickers of various kinds (if you provide them, people will use them!)
- ❏ X-Acto knife for cutting the box
- ❏ Stapler
- ❏ Toys—koosh balls, fun stuff, to keep the mood fun

Buy a Feature Materials (per table)

- ❏ Sample products (having a real product makes the game more effective; in the preceding example, you'd have a Blendz blender)
- ❏ Sufficient play money in prepackaged envelopes for each participant
- ❏ Lists of features

Start Your Day Materials

- ❏ Calendars in both normal and large-print formats

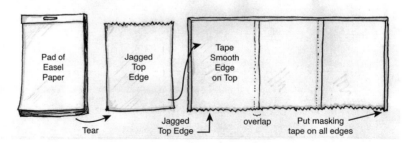

FIGURE 3.2 Put Easel Paper on Wall Surfaces

Table 3.3   Materials You Will Need to Supply

	Item	Purpose
❏	Thank you gifts for participants	
❏	Prizes	Optional item. Helps get creative juices flowing—such as a prize for the best product box.
❏	Place cards	Place cards contribute a sense of purpose and elegance to the event. More importantly, they are a subtle way to let you control seating. Prepare place cards as shown in Figure 3.3.

FIGURE 3.3 Prepare Place Cards

	Item	Purpose
❏	High-resolution digital camera	Enables your Bad Wedding Photographer to take lots of photos.
❏	50 5"×8" cards per observer	Provides your observers with everything they need to capture their observations.
❏	Markers	Provides your observers with everything that they need to capture their observations.
❏	Masking tape (various widths)	You'll want to tape things to the wall. Having a variety of widths makes it easy to choose the width that you need.
❏	Clear tape	Note that you'll need to bring more tape for certain games, such as *Product Box*. Err on the side of caution and bring more than you think you need.
❏	Clear super glue	
❏	Clear white glue	
❏	Small package of push pins	
❏	Music speakers and CDs	Theaters use "house lights" to signal when it is time to take your seat. You can use music in the same way. At the beginning of the event, during breaks, and during lunch, music can impart a special energy to the session.
❏	Air sanitizer or air freshener	Meeting rooms can sometimes acquire a musty or unpleasant odor. Having a can of air sanitizer or air freshener can help make the game experience more enjoyable.

Frequently Asked Questions (FAQs)

Here is list of common questions and their responses, in no particular order:

Games? How Do I Win?

This question can be asked by people preparing for an Innovation Game or by someone who is playing a game. If you're preparing for an Innovation Game, relax. Although we use the terminology of a game, the goal isn't "winning." It is *understanding*. You'll win in the marketplace when you understand how to create more innovative, profitable, and sustainable products and services.

If you're a facilitator and you receive this question from a customer, treat it as a rare gift, because it is a signal that they are buying into the process and that they want to "play" the game the right way. Simply say that the goal of the game really isn't winning, even if you're offering a prize for the best product box or the most interesting spider web. Instead, the goal is to have fun exploring and discussing how they see your product.

Do You Really Expect Me to Do This with Customers?

Yes. And you won't regret it. If you're really worried about playing a given game, choose a game that provides for less open-ended exploration (such as *Buy a Feature*), geared for relatively small numbers of customers (such as *Show and Tell*), or focus on product-related knowledge (such as *Start Your Day*). As you gain confidence, choose games that increase the degree of open-ended exploration and play the games with more customers.

Will My Customers Participate?

Our experience is that most customers enthusiastically respond to these games and participate with an open mind and a strong commitment to your success. The key word is *most*. There are customers who don't like the format of a given game or are uncomfortable working in small groups. The best way to handle this is through your selection process. Provide customers with enough information on your plans for using these games so that they can opt out if they are uncomfortable with the idea of participating directly with other customers in a form of qualitative market research.

What if Something Goes Wrong Before or During the Game?

Unexpected events often occur during a game, and sometimes they can be somewhat scary. Materials aren't delivered on time, and you have to make a midnight run to Walgreen's or Kinko's to scrape together whatever you can. An irate customer demands that you address their issues in real-time. Competitors refuse to participate because of concerns that they might inadvertently divulge confidential and/or proprietary data.

Although it is impossible to plan for every possibility, it is true that these unexpected events can cause real problems. The best approach when something unexpected happens is to maintain your professionalism and focus on your primary goals for playing the game. Then, adjust in real-time as necessary—change the game, ask another member of your team to privately handle an irate customer, put competitors into different groups, and so forth. Although the situation may be tense, at Enthiosys we have found that the majority of participants want to help you produce a good outcome and will be quite understanding and helpful when something does go wrong.

I'm Not a "Creative Type" and I'm Somewhat Shy. Can I Use These Techniques?

Absolutely. The primary criteria for using these techniques is a sincere desire to understand your customers. More importantly, a well-structured Innovation Game team has many roles where being shy is a virtue. Two that come to mind are the helper and observer, as neither of them require direct interaction with customers.

Our Company Has Never Run a Customer Event or User Group. What Happens if Customers Talk with Each Other?

In the modern world of the blogosphere and Web 2.0, chances are good that your customers are already talking about your products and services. That said, if you really are worried about what your customers might say when they get together in a group, you've got bigger issues than developing better customer understanding. Handle these issues before engaging an Innovation Game.

I've Identified People to Invite. How Do I Invite Them?

We recommend contacting them in a manner that works for your organization. If you're dealing with a small number of large accounts or major customers, chances are

---

This Is a Dumb Marketing Exercise!

I had just finished explaining the *Product Box* game to a group of participants when one of them exclaimed, "This is a dumb marketing exercise." Clearly, this was not the way I would have liked to start the process, especially since this was one of my client's largest and most prestigious customers, someone who had the ability to clearly influence other participants.

I took a deep breath and explained to the group that the game was a marketing exercise—one that we hoped would help us better understand their needs for a new product that was being developed. I asked the skeptical customer to "go with the flow" and prepare a box. He grunted, clearly unhappy with the concept of helping marketing, and set to work. I'm glad he

did. He created one of the session's best boxes, full of useful insights for the product and marketing teams.

I'd like to say this story has a completely happy ending, but it doesn't. Several senior executives were in the room, and although the product and marketing teams told them that the event produced extremely valuable results, some of the executives could remember only the initial negative response from an influential customer. As a result, it took time before this team felt comfortable running another game. Eventually, they did, taking special care to select and prepare participants for the experience. This produced better results for everyone involved.

good that you can leverage your customer service and/or account management organization. If you're dealing with a large number of small accounts and/or customers, we recommend traditional phone solicitation techniques to invite customers who meet your target profile.

Do I Need to Offer Participants Money to Attend?

This is a tough question with no clear-cut answer. The primary reason for offering money is that it is a clear signal that you respect your customers' time and participation in your event and that you want to make it easy for them to attend. The primary reason against offering money is that you want your customers to participate in the event because they are motivated to help you improve your products and services because doing so helps them do their job better. We tend to see companies paying for customer participation more frequently in business-to-consumer markets (B2C), for low-cost products or services, or for commodity services. We tend to see less of a need to pay for customer participation in business-to-business (B2B) and business-to-professional (B2P) markets, when the products are high cost, or when they are highly specialized.

We recommend giving participants a small token of your appreciation for their participation upon completion of the game. This "small token" is often relative to the amount of money customers spend on your products and services. In the B2C market, a small token might be an inexpensive clock or nice golf shirt. In the B2B market we've seen "small tokens" worth several hundred dollars

(a golf bag with custom embroidering was perhaps the most expensive item I've ever seen). In some of the games, such as *Product Box*, you may consider offering a prize for the most innovative box.

The key trick to making a gift work for your customers is tailoring the gift to their interests. One book reviewer commented that he thinks clocks are "cheesy" and that a golf-related gift would be "useless" as he doesn't play golf. He's right. If you're going to give a gift, it has to be thoughtfully chosen and have meaning.

I've Just Finished an Innovation Game and I'm Overwhelmed with the Amount of Data I Collected. Help!

Don't panic. We've found that people who are new to Innovation Games usually underestimate the amount of data that will be generated and the time necessary to postprocess the results into a useful format. If you feel overwhelmed by the amount of data you generated, consider processing it in two steps. Do a quick pass over the results to gather the most important themes. We typically do this immediately after a session. Then do a second, more thorough, review of the data to confirm the themes that you have identified.

Do I Have to Be a "Cool Creative Person" to Use Innovation Games?

No. You do not have to be a "creative type," a "smooth talker," or an unusually outgoing, extroverted person to use Innovation Games. The only requirement for playing Innovation Games is a sincere desire to better understand your customers and a willingness to try a new approach.

FACILITATING A TERRIFIC INNOVATION GAME SESSION

Not every person is an excellent facilitator, so here are some additional tips on how you can facilitate a terrific innovation game.

Your Goal: Understanding

Remember that your primary goal is to gain a better understanding of your customers. In terms of being an excellent facilitator, this means relying on proven facilitation techniques such as listening without prejudice, resisting the urge to lead the discussion, and avoiding justifying past decisions or making commitments about future products. Being a good facilitator can be pretty hard, especially when irate customers are venting their frustrations or unrealistic customers are asking for things that you, and often they, know just can't be done given the technologies or resources at your disposal. Try to keep in mind that customers who agree to participate in an Innovation Game have self-selected themselves as customers who are committed to your mutual success.

Practice Before You Play

Some of the Innovation Games profiled in this book, such as *Product Box*, *Show and Tell*, or *The Apprentice*, are pretty easy to facilitate. Others, such as *Remember the Future*, *Me and My Shadow*, or, *Give Them a Hot Tub*, are a bit harder, typically because they have more challenging preparation requirements. The phrase "practice makes perfect" applies, and if you're at all unsure of a technique, make certain you try it out with an internal team or a forgiving group of customers before going live. You'll feel better after you've practiced.

Allow Plenty of Time for the Session

As I was writing this book, I tried several times to figure out a few hard-and-fast rules to help you estimate how much time you'll need for each game. And I can't. The amount of time you'll need depends on far too many variables. Which game? How many customers are playing? How many games? How will you facilitate the game? Will you let customers talk as long as they want or will you hold them to a tight schedule? But completely copping out doesn't seem like a particularly good idea, either. So, instead of hard-and-fast rules, here are a few guidelines that have served me well:

- For groups of between 3 to 12 participants, plan on no more than two games per half-day session, with each game taking *at least* 90 minutes.
- For groups larger than 12 participants, plan on one game per half day.

Give yourself plenty of time during the game. Rush and you'll miss important things. Observing your customers may sound easy, but it isn't. Breathe. Be patient.

Give Customers Time to Play the Game

One of the worst things that you can do is ask your customers to play one of these games and then badger them into starting the exercise immediately. Give them a break. Most of the time, these games are such a radical departure from traditional meeting or focus group design that your customers are struggling to figure out if they're on the right planet, let alone in the right meeting! After you introduce a game, give your customers some time to think about what you have asked them to do. Remain available to answer their questions, remain observant for anyone who might appear stuck, but mostly, learn to be patient.

Quality, Not Quantity

You won't get any points if you play five games in one day but are so rushed and hurried that you fail to thoroughly explore the detailed information that customers will inevitably provide. Focus on quality. One exercise done well will provide you with a wealth of information. And because you're committed to your customers, you're going to be doing more of these games in the future. There is no need to rush, right?

Play Quiet Music

Consider playing quiet music in the background while participants are working. Contemporary, upbeat jazz, piano music, or Mozart works well, provided it isn't too loud. During breaks and lunch, turn up the volume and inject energy into the room with a mix of popular music. The music will provide an important set of auditory cues that will reinforce your agenda and the games that you're conducting. Like gifts, keep in mind that musical selections are highly personal, and while you may love country, others love rap and hip-hop. Stay relatively neutral in your selections and be prepared to change styles based on customer feedback.

Email Can Wait

When your customers are working, don't open your laptop or futz with your PDA. These can wait. Your customers can't. Remember that you need to actually write something on the blank 5"×8" cards that you've brought to capture your observations for later review. If you're doing email or playing a game on your PDA, you're not observing. And because customers can tell the difference, they'll actually start to act differently: Why should they give you their feedback if you're clearly not interested in the same?

Uh-oh...I Didn't Expect That

Innovation Games often evolve in unexpected ways. That's part of the fun. Indeed, a well-facilitated game is actually a bit chaotic. If you're the kind of person who has trouble "going with the flow" with a customer, think carefully about attempting to facilitate an Innovation Game. Consider, instead, a different role on the team.

Transcribe the Results

Even with high-resolution photos, it is best to transcribe everything that customers create. This makes postprocessing game results easier because you can move, group, and search text. It also makes it easier to find key phrases from customers when searching documents.

Give Them Feedback

They were kind enough to participate in your exercises, so you can be kind enough to provide them with a copy of your final report. Therefore, you should create two reports: an external report, complete with digital photos of the event, for sharing with customers and an internal report, with the observations and commentary of your team, highlighting how the results of the Innovation Game will be incorporated into your product and service development efforts.

Say Thank You

You don't have to pay them or bribe them with lavish gifts, although a token of your appreciation can make the event meaningful. You do need to say "Thank you" when the event is over, no matter what they've told you. And mean it when you say it, because if you don't, they'll know.

Customize with Experience

Although you should feel comfortable in modifying these techniques to meet specific needs, avoid this until you've gained experience in the techniques as they are presented.

A Good Facilitator

A good facilitator is someone who can laugh easily at themselves and the sometimes crazy situations that can happen when playing a game. Ground yourself in the belief that you will have fun, that you'll laugh and learn about what your customers really want—and you will. I look forward to reading in the forums about your experiences playing Innovation Games.

CONCLUSION

I first had the idea to write this book in the summer of 2003 when I was helping QUAL-COMM Wireless Business Solutions (QWBS) plan a sales training seminar. The seminar was unique because we were inviting customers to teach the sales team which part of the sales processes had actually worked. That wasn't going to take all day, so the QWBS planning team asked me, "What else can we do with our customers?"

Not surprisingly, I suggested that we use some of the informal games I had developed to better elicit customer needs and desires. As Joan Waltman described in her foreword, QWBS overcame their initial skepticism and obtained valuable insights from playing the games with their customers. I reflected on our experience, and thought that it contained the seed of what would be a useful book for people who want to better understand their customers. Hopefully, you'll agree.

More importantly, like the many people who work for companies that have committed themselves to creating market-leading innovations by better understanding their customers, I hope you'll see the end of this book as the beginning of your use of Innovation Games.

If I am ever fortunate enough to meet with you in your office, I look forward to seeing several product boxes on the top of your bookshelf right next to the spider webs and *Start Your Day* calendars hanging on your walls. Next to them, I hope to find photographs and rich descriptions of your customers from *Me and My Shadow* as I listen to you describe the customer artifacts you collected playing *Show and Tell*. Somewhere beneath all of these things I hope to see a worn and battered copy of *Innovation Games*, no longer needed because of the many games that you've played with your customers. Until then, I'll enjoy reading about your experiences in the Innovation Games forum at www.innovationgames.com.

Luke Hohmann

INDEX

A

action. *See* commitment to action
agenda example, 133-136
AIPMM (Association for International Product Marketing and Product Management), 53
AirTransportIT, 80
    customizing Innovation Games, 131-132
    sample thank you letter, 137, 140-141
Aladdin Knowledge Systems, Inc., 80, 120, 129
The Apprentice game, 2, 106-109
    Dogfooding versus, 109
    example of usage, 108
    Me and My Shadow game versus, 97
    playing, 108
    preparing for, 107-108
    processing results, 108-109
    reasons for using, 107
artwork. *See* customer artwork
Association for International Product Marketing and Product Management (AIPMM), 53

B

brainstorming, 103
Buy a Feature game, 3, 25, 76-83
    for CABs (Customer Advisory Boards), 45
    customizing, 132
    materials list, 142
    playing, 81-82
    preparing for, 77-81
    processing results, 82
    reasons for using, 77

C

CABs (Customer Advisory Boards), 44-45
Cares, James P., 17
checklists
    materials list, 142-143
    planning Innovation Games, 28
choosing. *See* selecting
closing meeting, 28
commitment to action
    from Innovation Games, 17
    in real-time, 19
    time frame for, 24-25
communication in Innovation Games, 17
complaints. *See* Speed Boat game
complex-systems architectures, statistics in, 12
context diagramming, 64
continuum of knowledge, 8
corporate relationships, 64
Customer Advisory Boards (CABs), 44-45
customer artwork, processing, 37
customer complaints. *See* Speed Boat game
customer preparation requirements, selecting Innovation Games, 24
customer relationship, 7
customer reports, preparing, 39-40
customer requirements, 7, 43
customer research. *See* market research
customer support, 7
Customer Visits: Building a Better Market Focus (McQuarrie), 43
customer-centric innovation, 7, 40-43
    ideation phase, 41-43
    market research versus, 40-41

Customer-Centric Product Definition (Mello), 43
customers
    benefits from Innovation Games, 27
    defining, 14
    empathy for. *See* The Apprentice game
    market segmentation, 12-13
    number needed for games, 21-22
    real-time commitment to action, 19
    selecting, 128
    single versus multiple for games, 94
customizing Innovation Games, 131-132

D

Dealing with Darwin (Moore), 12
design continuums, 112
details in Remember the Future game, 60
direct customers, 14
directed market research. *See* market research
Dogfooding, The Apprentice game versus, 109

E

Emerson Climate Technologies, 129
empathy for customers. *See*
           The Apprentice game
environmental relationships, 64
ethnographic research, 97
event planning. *See* planning
Extreme Data Sheet, 70

F

facilitators (team role), 31-32
    tips for, 147-148
FAQs (frequently asked questions), 144-146
feature retailers (team role), 81
features. *See* Buy a Feature game;
          20/20 Vision game
feedback. *See* customers

FIFA World Cup, 60
Finite and Infinite Games (Cares), 17
finite games, 17
"Five W's," 27-28, 128-130
Follow-Me-Home program (Intuit), 98

G–H

gated processes, 41
gifts for participants, 146
Give Them a Hot Tub game, 3, 102-105
    for CABs (Customer Advisory Boards), 45
    playing, 104
    preparing for, 103-104
    processing results, 104-105
    reasons for using, 103
greeters (team role), 30
Grossman, Glenn, 81

helpers (team role), 31
Highsmith, Jim, 70
human relationships, 65

I

ideation phase, 41-43
indirect customers, 14
individual knowledge, organizing, 8
infinite games, 17
Innovation Games. *See also names of*
          specific games
    combining, 95
    with Customer Advisory Boards (CABs),
        44-45
    customer benefits, 27
    for customer relationship, 7
    for customer requirements, 7, 43
    for customer-centric innovation, 7, 40-43
        ideation phase, 41-43
        market research versus, 40-41

customizing, 131-132

example of usage, 4-5

FAQs (frequently asked questions), 144-146

international appeal of, 72

list of, 2

for market research, 7

    acting on, 14-15

    defined, 7-9

    market segmentation, 12-13

    primary and secondary data, 10-12

    process of, 9-10

    qualitative market research, advantages of, 15

    questions to answer, 11

    simplistic versus complex approaches, 5

mentioning in invitations, 129

organizing, 6

planning, 26

    preparation phases, 27-29, 128-130

    setup for games, 3-37

    size of team, 35

    timeline for, 26-27

    using Remember the Future game, 26

processing results of, 37

    customer artwork, 37

    observer note cards, 38-39

    report preparation, 39-40

    retrospective, 39

process of, 18-20

sample agenda, 133-136

sample invitation letter, 137-138

sample thank you letter, 137-139

selecting, 20-25

    open-ended exploration, 21

    preparation requirements, 22-24

    scalability, 21-22

    time frame for action, 24-25

team roles, 29

    facilitators, 31-32, 147-148

    greeters, 30

    helpers, 31

    observers, 33-35

    organizers, 30

    photographers, 35

    planners, 29-30

    time requirements, 147

    unique advantages of, 16-18

internal reports, preparing, 39-40

international appeal of Innovation Games, 72

Intuit's Follow-Me-Home program, 98

invitations

    mentioning Innovation Games in, 129

    methods of inviting, 145

    sample letter, 137-138

    selecting customers to invite, 128

J–K–L

Kano analysis, 115

kickoff meetings, 28, 42

knowledge, continuum of, 8

Leffingwell, Dean, 70

legal issues, 130

location relationships, 64

M

market events, preparing for Start Your Day game, 88

market preparation requirements, selecting Innovation Games, 23

market research, 7. *See also* customers

    acting on, 14-15

    customer-centric innovation versus, 40-41

    customers, defining, 14

    defined, 7-9

    market segmentation, 12-13

    primary and secondary data, 10-12

    process of, 9-10

    qualitative data, 12

qualitative market research,
    advantages of, 15
questions to answer, 11
simplistic versus complex approaches, 5
unique advantages of Innovation Games,
    16-18
market rhythms, preparing for Start Your Day
    game, 88
market segmentation, 12-13
marketing exercise, Product Box game as, 145
master of ceremonies. *See* greeters (team role)
materials lists for games
    The Apprentice, 108
    basic checklist, 142-143
    Buy a Feature, 81, 142
    Give Them a Hot Tub, 104
    Me and My Shadow, 98
    Product Box, 71, 142
    Prune the Product Tree, 52
    Remember the Future, 59
    Show and Tell, 94
    Speed Boat, 120
    Spider Web, 65
    Start Your Day, 87, 142
    20/20 Vision, 112
Mayer, Tobias, 120
McQuarrie, Edward, 43
Me and My Shadow game, 2, 96-101
    The Apprentice game versus, 97
    playing, 98-100
    preparing for, 98
    processing results, 100
    reasons for using, 97-98
    videotaping, 99
Meeting Professionals International
    web site, 128
Mello, Sheila, 43
money for participants, 146
Moore, Geoffrey, 12
music during games, 148

N–O

negative economic attributes, 115
Newsom, Jef, 78
note cards, processing, 38-39

observer note cards, processing, 38-39
observers (team role), 33-35
open-ended exploration, selecting Innovation
    Games, 21
operating relationships, 64
organizers (team role), 30
organizing
    individual knowledge, 8
    Innovation Games, 6
Oriel, Inc., 43

P

Padilla, Therese, 53
Peacock, Steve, 120
phases of preparation for planning Innovation
    Games, 27-29, 128-130
photographers (team role), 35
physical preparation requirements, selecting
    Innovation Games, 22-23
planners (team role), 29-30
planning Innovation Games, 26. *See also*
    preparing for specific games
    preparation phases, 27-29, 128-130
    setup for games, 35-37
    size of team, 35
    timeline for, 26-27
    using Remember the Future game, 26
PMEC (Product Management Educational
    Conference), 53
positive economic attributes, 115
preparation phases for planning Innovation
    Games, 27-29, 128-130
preparation requirements, selecting Innovation
    Games, 22-24

preparing for specific games. *See also* planning
    Innovation Games
    The Apprentice, 107-108
    Buy a Feature, 77-81
    Give Them a Hot Tub, 103-104
    Me and My Shadow, 98
    Product Box, 69-72
    Prune the Product Tree, 49-52
    Remember the Future, 59
    Show and Tell, 93-94
    Speed Boat, 120
    Spider Web, 64-65
    Start Your Day, 86-87
    20/20 Vision, 112
pricing features for Buy a Feature game, 78
primary data, 10-12
priorities. *See* Speed Boat game;
    20/20 Vision game
problems, prioritizing. *See* Speed Boat game
Product Box game, 2, 25, 68-75
    for CABs (Customer Advisory Boards), 45
    customizing, 132
    as marketing exercise, 145
    materials list, 142
    playing, 72-73
    preparing for, 69-72
    processing results, 74-75
    reasons for using, 69-70
    using with Show and Tell game, 95
Product Management Educational Conference
    (PMEC), 53
product requirements. *See* customer
    requirements
product teams, involvement in Innovation
    Games, 16
professional facilitators, advantages of
    using, 32
project managers. *See* planners (team role)

Prune the Product Tree game, 2, 48-55
    example of usage, 53
    playing, 52-54
    preparing for, 49-52
    processing results, 54
    reasons for using, 49

Q

qualitative data, 12
qualitative market research, advantages of, 15.
    See also market research
Qualitative Research Consultants
    Association, 32
quantitative data, 12
questions
    framing for Remember the Future game,
      59-60
    for market research, 11

R

Rally Software Development, 137
real-time commitment to action, 19
relationships in Spider Web game, 64. *See also*
    customer relationship
Remember the Future game, 3, 56-61
    for CABs (Customer Advisory Boards), 45
    example of usage, 58-60
    planning Innovation Games with, 26
    playing, 59-61
    preparing for, 59
    processing results, 61
    reasons for using, 57-59
    using with Show and Tell game, 95
remote control exercise, 65
reports, preparing, 39-40
requirements. *See* customer requirements

results, processing, 37
    The Apprentice game, 108-109
    Buy a Feature game, 82
    customer artwork, 37
    Give Them a Hot Tub game, 104-105
    Me and My Shadow game, 100
    observer note cards, 38-39
    overwhelming nature of, 146
    Product Box game, 74-75
    Prune the Product Tree game, 54
    Remember the Future game, 61
    report preparation, 39-40
    retrospective, 39
    Show and Tell game, 95
    Speed Boat game, 123-124
    Spider Web game, 66
    Start Your Day game, 89-90
    20/20 Vision game, 114-116
retrospective (processing results), 39
role relationships, 65

S

Samana Nacional PyME, 72
sample agenda, 133-136
sample invitation letter, 137-138
sample thank you letters, 137, 139-141
scalability, selecting Innovation Games, 21-22
secondary data, 10-12
segmentation. *See* market segmentation
selecting
    customers to invite, 128
    Innovation Games, 20-25
        open-ended exploration, 21
        preparation requirements, 22-24
        scalability, 21-22
        time frame for action, 24-25
Show and Tell game, 2, 92-95
    for CABs (Customer Advisory Boards), 45
    playing, 95

preparing for, 93-94
processing results, 95
reasons for using, 93
single versus multiple customers
    participating, 94
using with other Innovation Games, 95
silence during games, handling, 148
Smith, Dave, 58
SOFA (Systematic, Objective, Focused,
    Actionable), 9
Speed Boat game, 3, 25, 118-125
    customizing, 131
    playing, 121-123
    preparing for, 120
    processing results, 123-124
    reasons for using, 119-120
Spider Web game, 3, 25, 62-67
    playing, 66
    preparing for, 64-65
    processing results, 66
    reasons for using, 63-64
splitting customer groups in 20/20 Vision
    game, 113
Start Your Day game, 2, 84-91
    for CABs (Customer Advisory Boards), 45
    materials list, 142
    playing, 88-89
    preparing for, 86-87
    processing results, 89-90
    reasons for using, 86
    using with Show and Tell game, 95
statistics in complex-systems architectures, 12
support. *See* customer relationship

T

team roles, 29
    facilitators, 31-32, 147-148
    greeters, 30
    helpers, 31

observers, 33-35

organizers, 30

photographers, 35

planners, 29-30

size of team, 35

thank you letter examples, 139-141

time frame for action, selecting Innovation
Games, 24-25

timeline for planning Innovation Games, 26-27

time requirements

Innovation Games, 147

processing results of Innovation Games, 37

trees. *See* Prune the Product Tree game

20/20 Vision game, 3, 110-117

playing, 112-114

preparing for, 112

processing results, 114-116

reasons for using, 111

U–Z

unexpected events, handling, 144

unintended uses of products, 89

universal remote control exercise, 65

videotaping for Me and My Shadow game, 99

Vision Box, 70

*Voices into Choices: Acting on the Voice of the
Customer* (Oriel, Inc.), 43

winning the game, 144

Register
Your Book

at www.awprofessional.com/register

You may be eligible to receive:

- **Advance notice of forthcoming editions of the book**
- **Related book recommendations**
- **Chapter excerpts and supplements of forthcoming titles**
- **Information about special contests and promotions throughout the year**
- **Notices and reminders about author appearances, tradeshows, and online chats with special guests**

Contact us

If you are interested in writing a book or reviewing manuscripts prior to publication, please write to us at:

Editorial Department
Addison-Wesley Professional
75 Arlington Street, Suite 300
Boston, MA 02116 USA
Email: AWPro@aw.com

Visit us on the Web: http://www.awprofessional.com

Prune the Product Tree

Shape Your Product to Market Needs

Remember the Future

*Understand Your Customers'
Definition of Success*

Spider Web

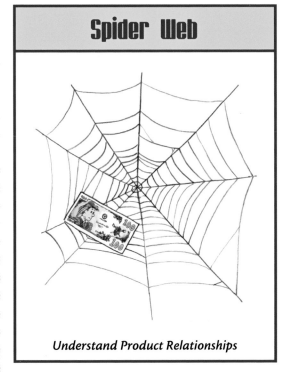

Understand Product Relationships

Product Box

Identify the Most Exciting Product Features

Remember the Future

GOAL: Understand your customers' definition of success

ACTIVITY: Hand each of your customers a few pieces of paper. Ask them to imagine that it is sometime in the future and that they've been using your product almost continuously between now and that future date (it could be a month, quarter, year, or, for strategic planning purposes, five years or even a decade—pick a time frame that is appropriate for your research goals). Now, ask them to go even further—an extra day, week, month. Ask your customer to write down, in as much detail as possible, exactly what your product will have done to make them happy (or successful or rich or safe or secure or smart; choose the set of adjectives that works best for your product).

Note: The phrasing of the question is extremely important. You'll get different results if you ask "What should the system do?" instead of "What will the system have done?" (If you're skeptical, just try it.)

Prune the Product Tree

GOAL: Shape your product to market needs

ACTIVITY: Start by drawing a large tree on a whiteboard or butcher paper or printing a graphic image of a tree as a large format poster. Thick limbs represent major areas of functionality within your system. The inside of the tree contains leaves that represent features in the current release. Leaves that are placed at the outer edge of the canopy represent new features. The edge of the tree represents the future. Write potential new features on several index cards, ideally shaped as leaves. Ask your customers to place desired features around the tree, shaping its growth. Do they structure a tree that is growing in a balanced manner? Does one branch, perhaps a core feature of the product, get the bulk of the growth? Does an underutilized aspect of the tree become stronger? We know that the roots of a tree (your support and customer care infrastructure) need to extend at least as far as its canopy. Do yours?

Product Box

GOAL: Identify the most exciting product features

ACTIVITY: Ask your customers to imagine that they're selling your product at a trade show, retail outlet, or public market. Give them a few blank white cardboard boxes and ask them to design the product box that they would buy. The box can contain anything they want—marketing slogans that they find interesting, pictures, price points. They can build elaborate boxes through the materials you provide or just write down the phrases and slogans they find most interesting. When finished, ask your customer to use *their* box to sell *your product* to *you* and the other customers in the room. What happens when they do this? Which of your customers want to buy this box? Why?

Spider Web

GOAL: Understand product relationships

ACTIVITY: Put the name or an image of your product or service in the center of a large flip chart or blank poster hung on a wall. Ask your customers to draw other things they think are related to your offering. These things can be other products or services, companies, people, physical objects, or locations—anything they think is important. Encourage them to use different colors, line weights, or styles to capture important relationships, such as a thick line for important relationships or a gold line for beneficial relationships. When finished, ask your customers to explain their drawing to the group.

Buy a Feature

Prioritize Features

Start Your Day

Understand When and How Your Customer Uses Your Product

Show and Tell

Identify the Most Important Artifacts Created by Your Product

Me and My Shadow

Identify Your Customers' Hidden Needs

Start Your Day

GOAL: Understand when and how your customer uses your product

ACTIVITY: On preprinted, poster-sized calendars or on a simple timeline drawn on a large sheet of paper, ask your customers to describe the daily, weekly, monthly, and yearly activities that are related to their use of your product. Ask them to describe activities in time frames appropriate for your product—beginnings and ends of days or weeks, recurring events such as birthdays, one-time activities such as installing a new software system, special activities that are unique to an industry or sector (like a conference), or days in which everything goes horribly wrong and they're looking for help. While they're doing this, be alert for how your product helps, or hinders, their day.

Buy a Feature

GOAL: Prioritize features

ACTIVITY: Create a list of potential features and provide each with a price. Just like for a real product, the price can be based on development costs, customer value, or something else. Although the price can be the actual cost you intend to charge for the feature, this is usually not required. Customers buy features that they want in the next release of your product using play money you give them. Make certain that some features are priced high enough that no one customer can buy them. Encourage customers to pool their money to buy especially important and/or expensive features. This will help motivate negotiations between customers as to which features are most important. This game works best with four to seven customers in a group, so that you can create more opportunities for customers to pool their money through negotiating.

Me and My Shadow

GOAL: Identify your customers' hidden needs

ACTIVITY: Shadow your customers while they use your product or service. Literally. Sit or stand next to them and watch what they do. Periodically ask them, "Why are you doing that?" and "What are you thinking?" Take along a camera and make photos of key activities and the context in which work is accomplished. Ask for copies of important artifacts created or used by your customers while they are doing the work. Bring along other customers and use them as interpreters to explain what a customer is doing, help you ask clarifying questions as to why the customer is doing things this way. During the game, ask your other customers to share whether they do things the same way with the person you're observing, and watch how your customers explore and even debate the various approaches they bring to using your products and services.

Me and My Shadow differs from *The Apprentice* in that *Me and My Shadow* focuses on observation and *The Apprentice* focuses on experience.

Show and Tell

GOAL: Identify the most important artifacts created by your product

ACTIVITY: Ask your customers to bring examples of artifacts created or modified by your product or service. Ask them to tell you why these artifacts are important and when and how they're used. For example, if your product is a software system to manage invoices, ask them to show you the invoices, reports, or spreadsheets that they've created through using your product. If you make running shoes, ask your customers to bring you several pairs of worn shoes and tell you about how they become so worn (maybe it is not from running).

Pay careful attention to anything that surprises you. What did you expect customers to create or modify that they have ignored? What things can you do with your product or service that aren't used? What was used in unexpected ways? What do these tell you?

Give Them a Hot Tub

*Use Outrageous Features to
Discover Hidden Breakthroughs*

The Apprentice

Create Empathy for the Customer Experience

20/20 Vision

Understand Customer Priorities

Speed Boat

*Identify What Customers Don't Like
About Your Product or Service*

The Apprentice

GOAL: Create empathy for the customer experience
ACTIVITY: Ask your development team to perform the "work" of the system that they are building. If they're creating a new masking tape for painters, ask them to work with real painters, using the masking tape in the field. If they're creating a new professional oven, ask them to cook meals with a professional chef—not in a classroom, but in a real restaurant, where they have to experience the actual challenges of creating meals. If they're building workflow management software for furniture delivery people, have them deliver furniture. They will gain direct knowledge of the problems customers face and empathy for how hard it may be to solve them.

Give Them a Hot Tub

GOAL: Use outrageous features to discover hidden breakthroughs
ACTIVITY: Write several features on note cards, one feature per card. Some of these features should seem normal. Others should be outrageous. For example, if you're making a portable MP3 player, try adding features like "heats coffee," "cracks concrete," or "conditions dog hair." If you're making a system that manages payroll, try adding features like "plans family reunions" or "refinishes wooden floors." If you're building an office building, add a hot tub in the lobby. Present each feature to your customers one at a time. How do customers react to the normal features? How do they react to the outrageous features?

Speed Boat

GOAL: Identify what customers don't like about your product or service
ACTIVITY: Draw a boat on a whiteboard or sheet of butcher paper. You'd like the boat to really move fast. Unfortunately, the boat has a few anchors holding it back. The boat is your system, and the features that your customers don't like are its anchors.

Customers write what they don't like on an index card and place it under the boat as an anchor. They can also estimate how much faster the boat would go if that anchor were cut and add that to the card. Estimates of speed are really estimates of pain. Customers can also annotate the anchors created by other customers, indicating agreement on substantial topics. When customers are finished posting their anchors, review each one, carefully confirming your understanding of what they want to see changed in the system.

20/20 Vision

GOAL: Understand customer priorities
ACTIVITY: When you're getting fitted for glasses, your optometrist will often ask you to compare two potential lenses by alternately showing each of them. Although it may take some time, eventually you'll settle on the set of lenses that are best for your eyes. You can use a variant of this approach to help your customers see which priorities are best for them.

Start by writing one feature each on large index cards. Shuffle the pile and put them face down. Take the first one from the top of the pile and put it on the wall. Take the next one and ask your customers if it is more or less important than the one on the wall. If it is more important, place it higher. If it is less important, put it lower. Repeat this process with all your feature cards, and you'll develop 20/20 vision for what your market really wants.